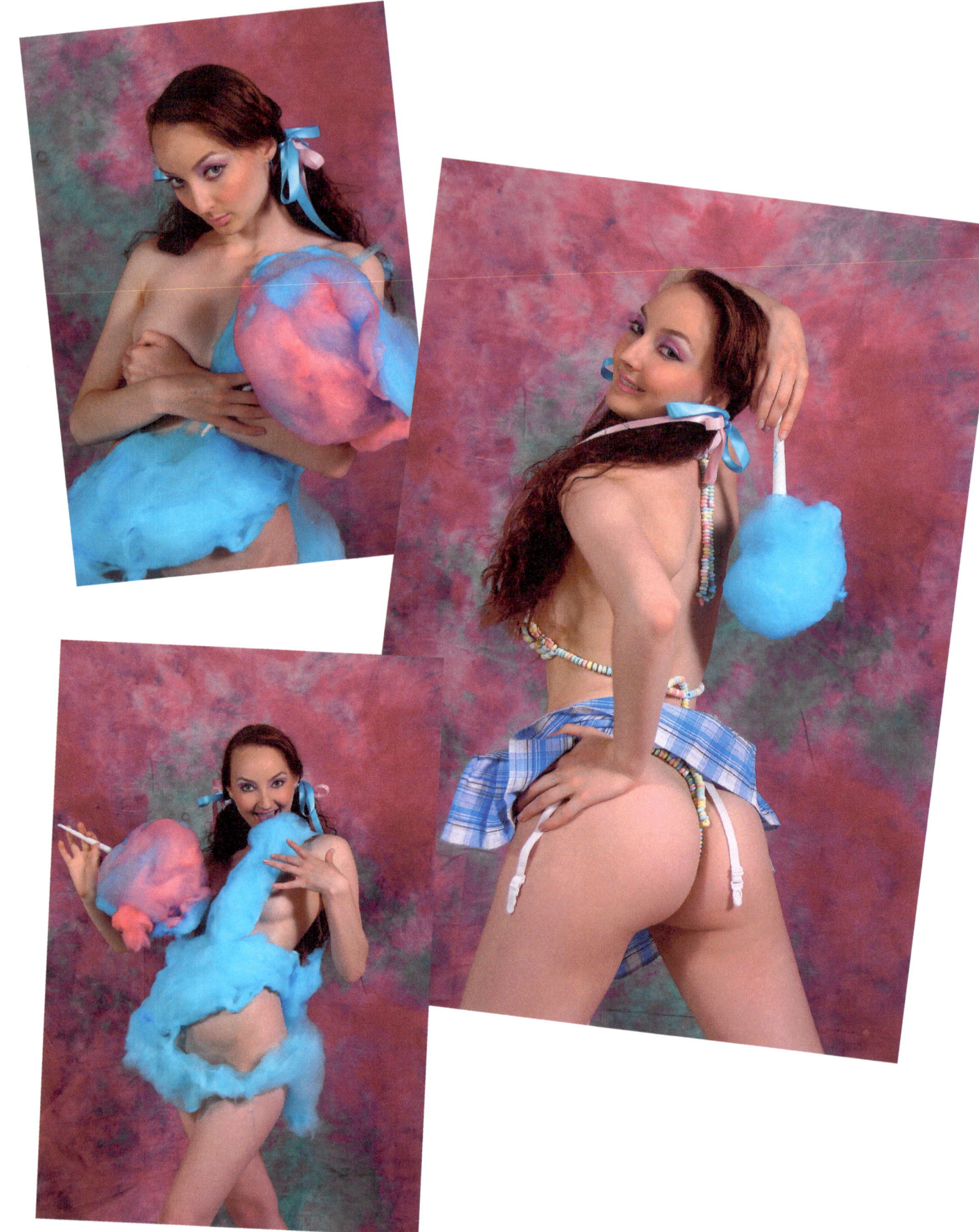

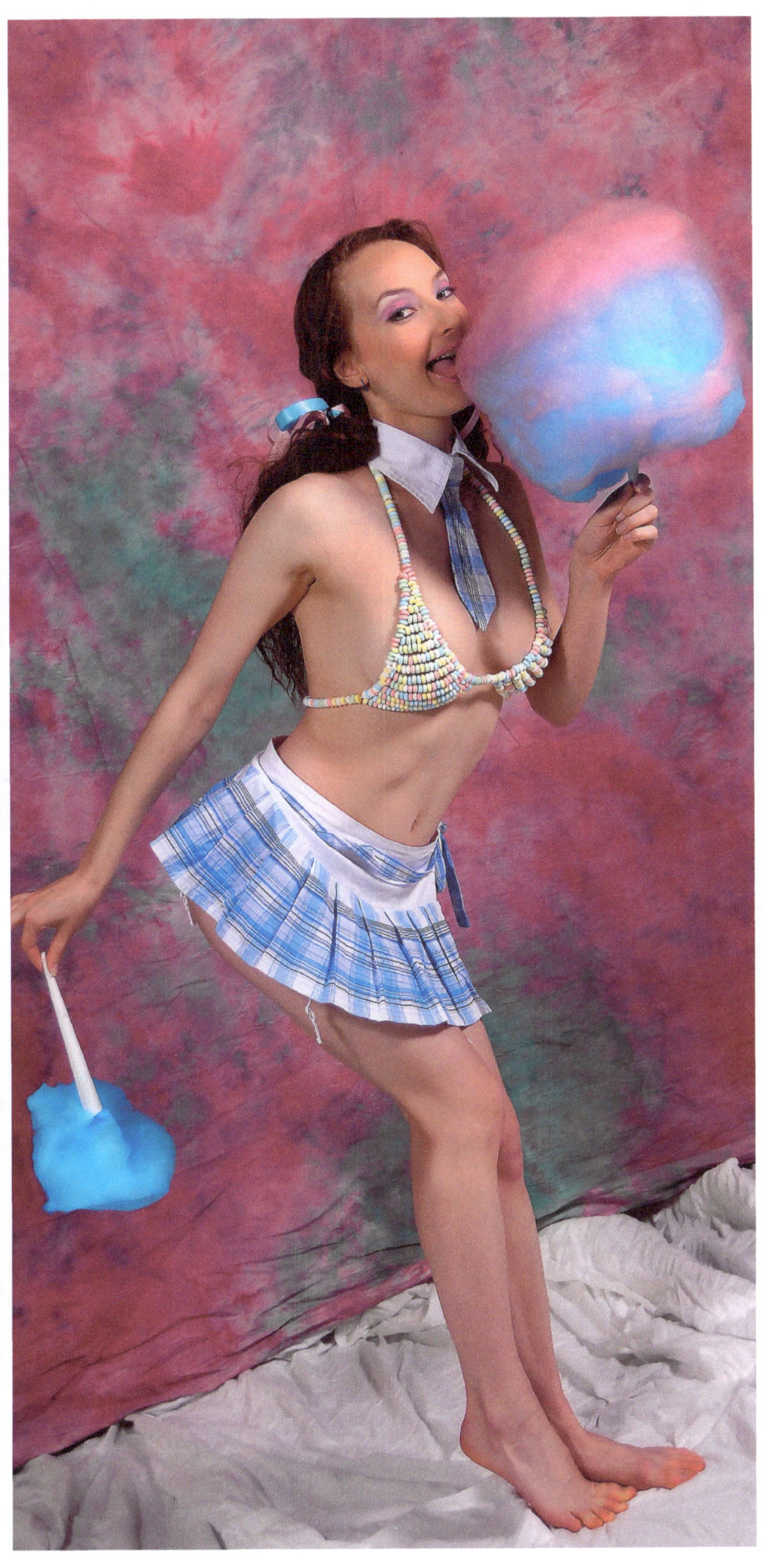

Sydeline Sweeties
BrittaniLuv

Ordering Information:

Tia Tormen Productions
P.O. Box 8069
Pittsburgh, PA 15216

Contact tiatormen@yahoo.com

Printed in the
United States of America

ISBN-10:0985935421

ISBN-13:978-0-9859354-2-9

First Edition

All Women
Are Beautiful

Some Women
Grab Your Imagination
And Never Let Go !

Introducing:
Brittani Luv

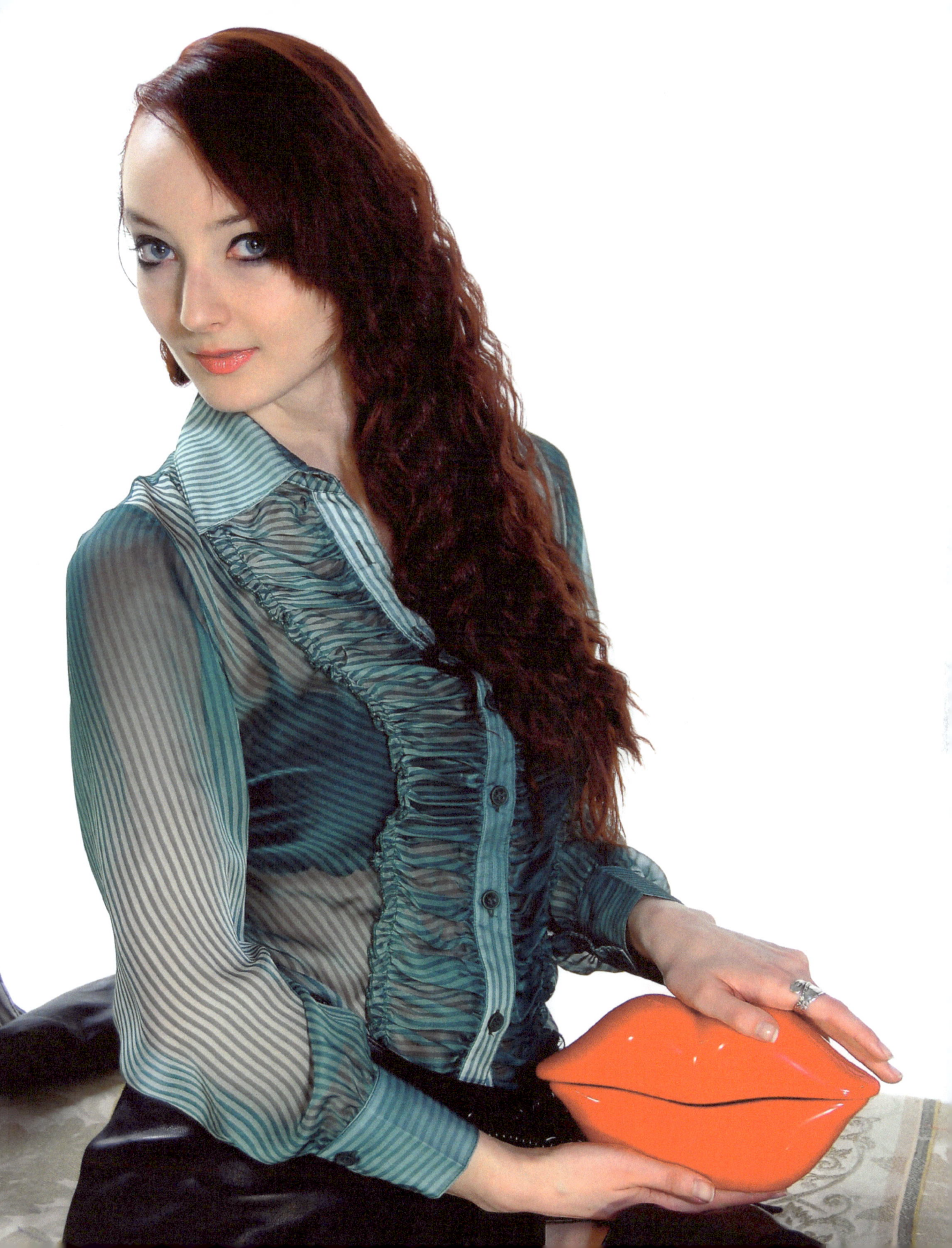

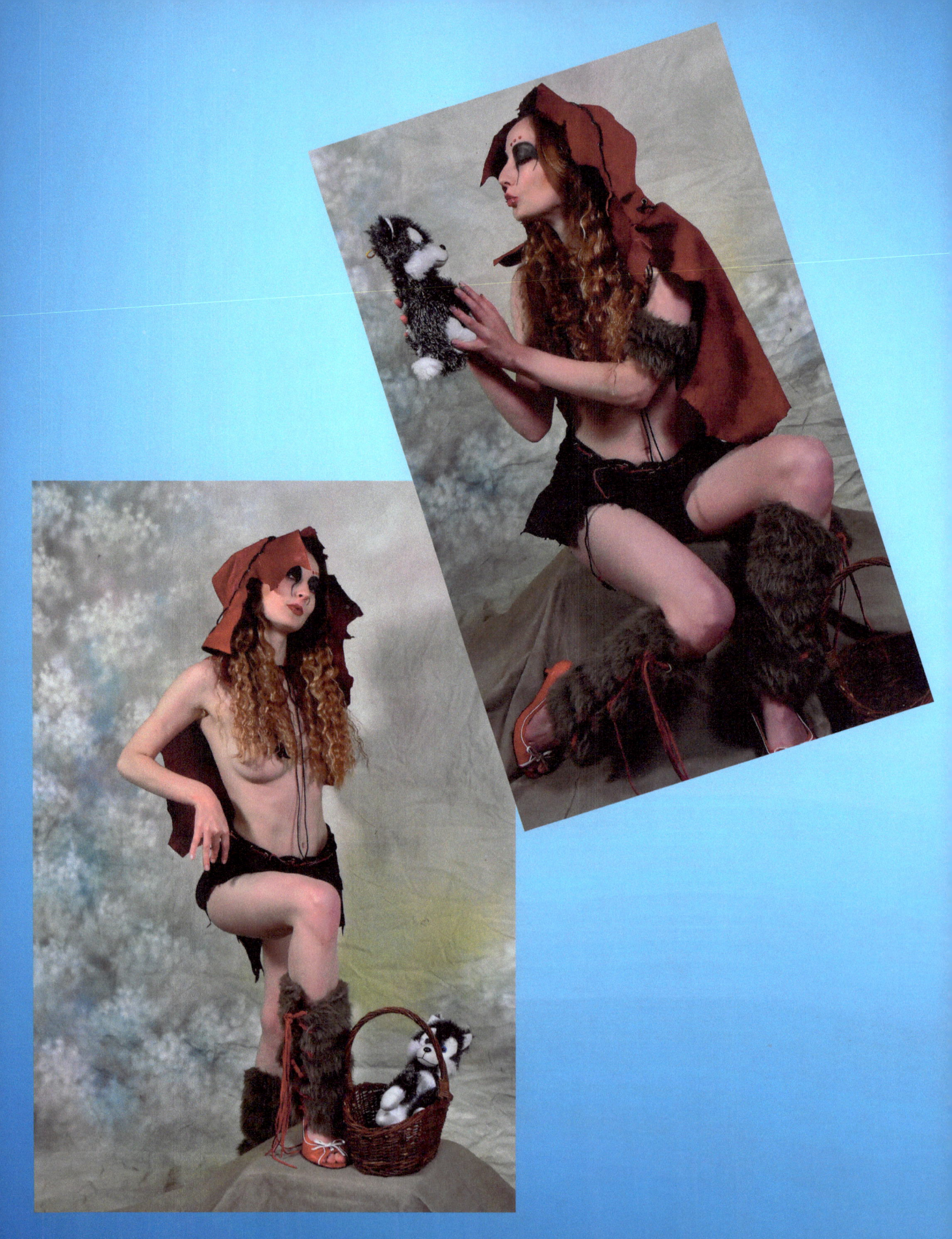

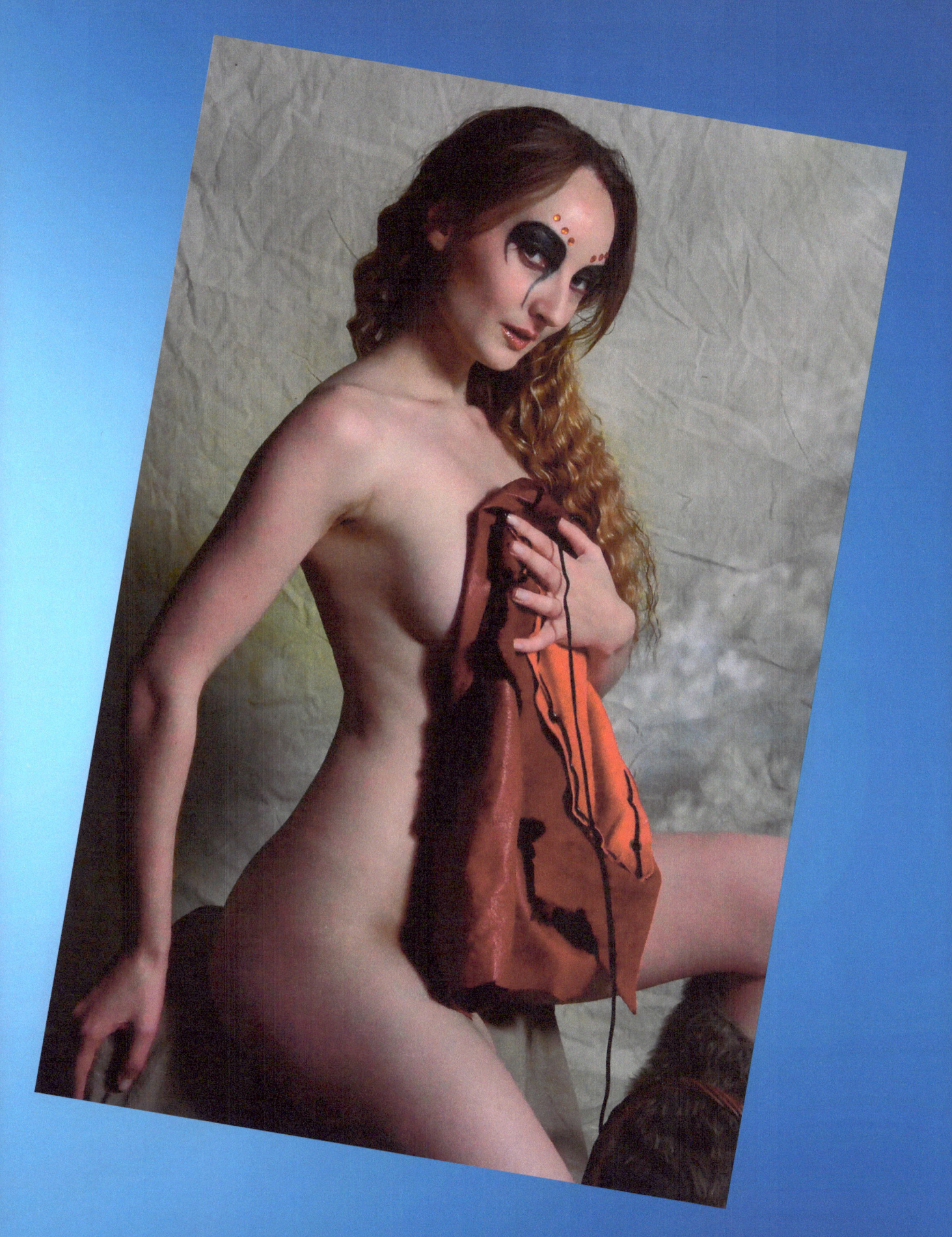

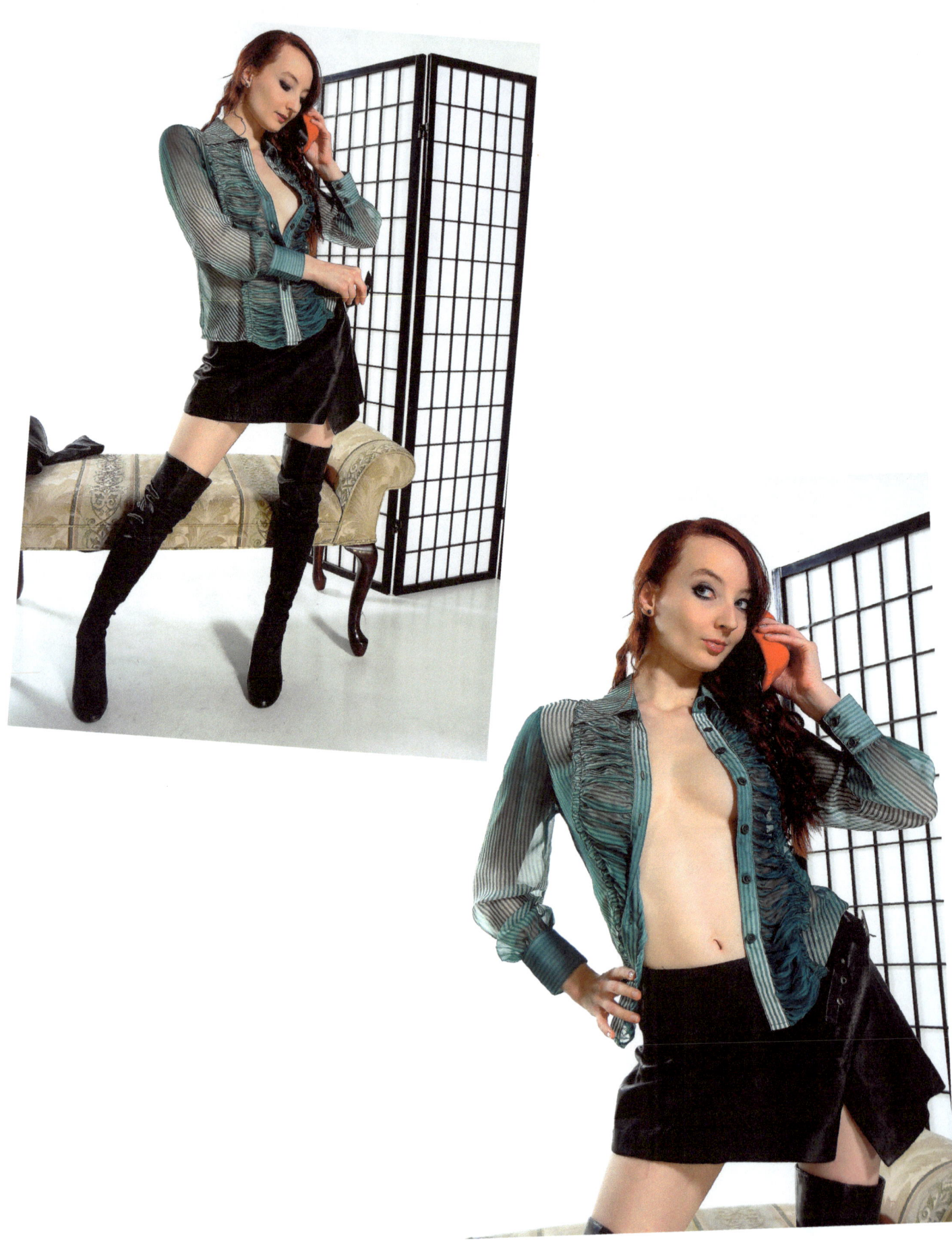

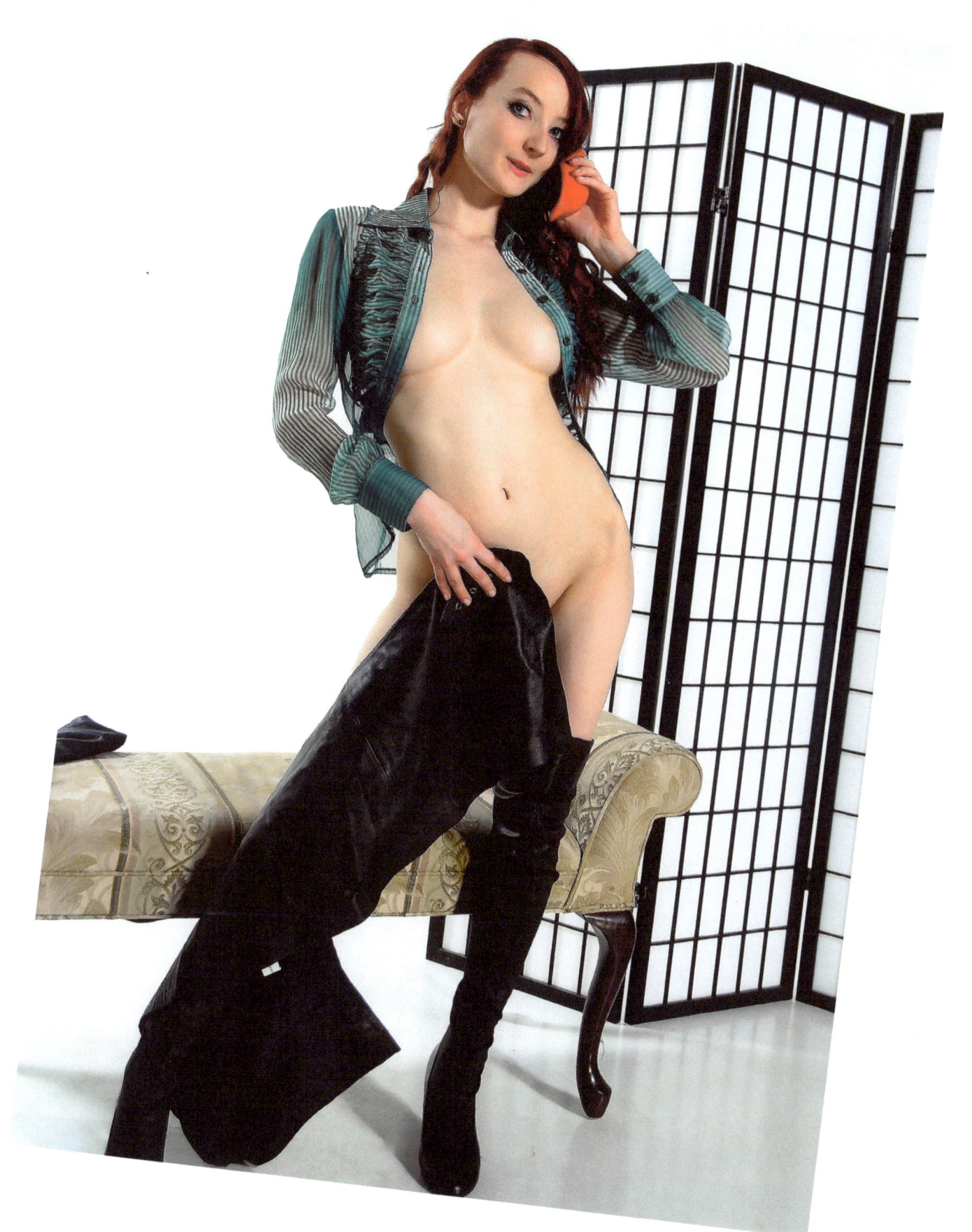

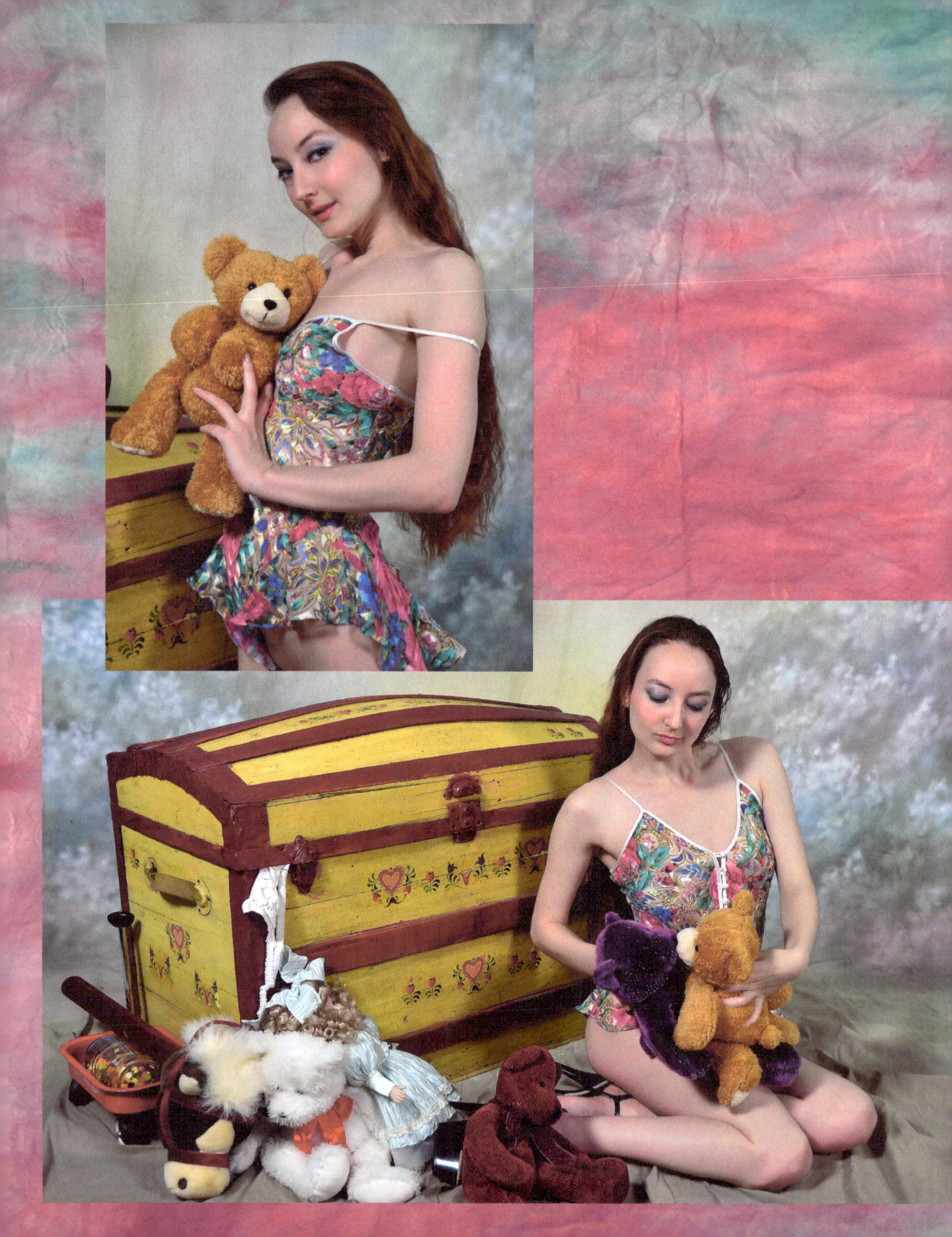

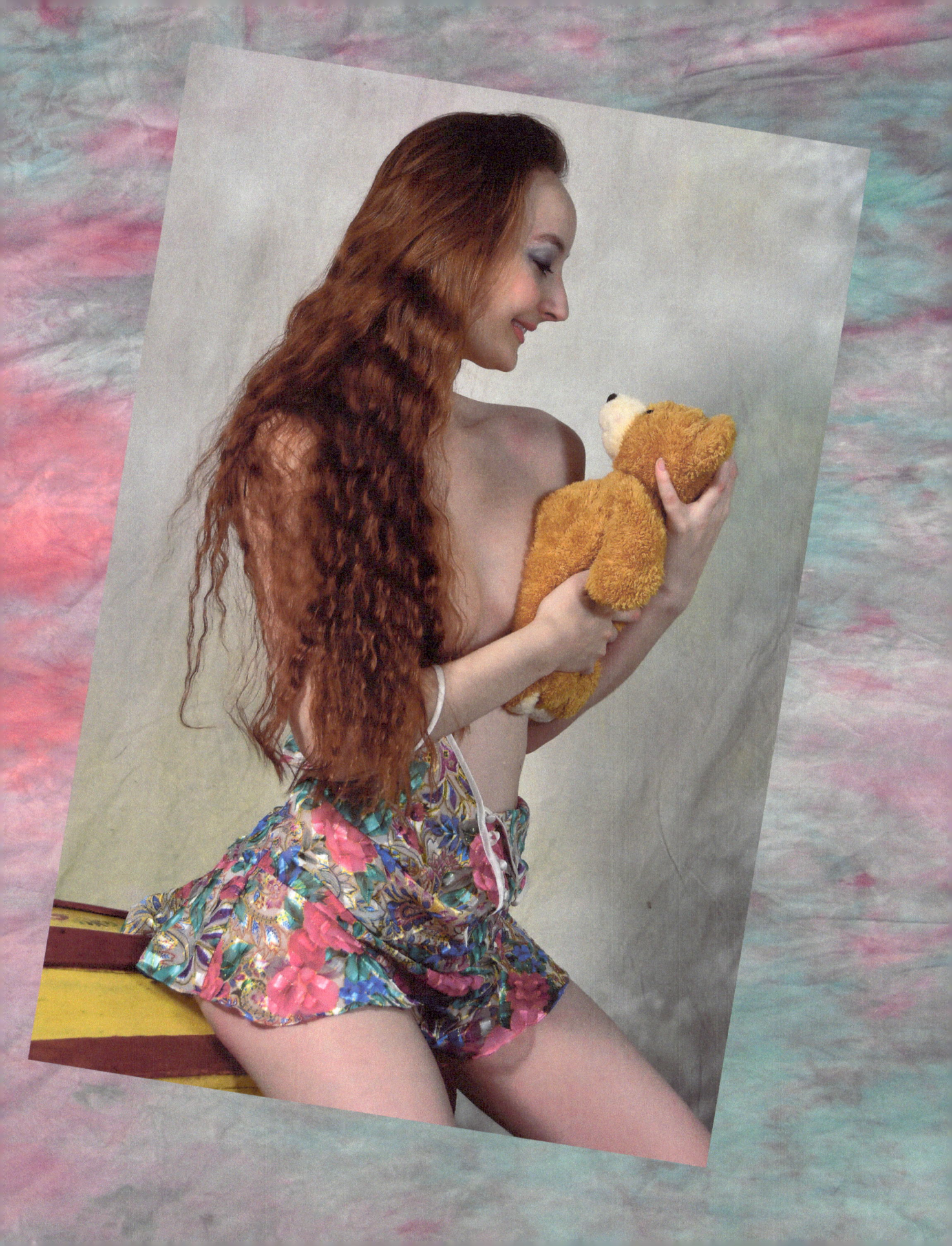

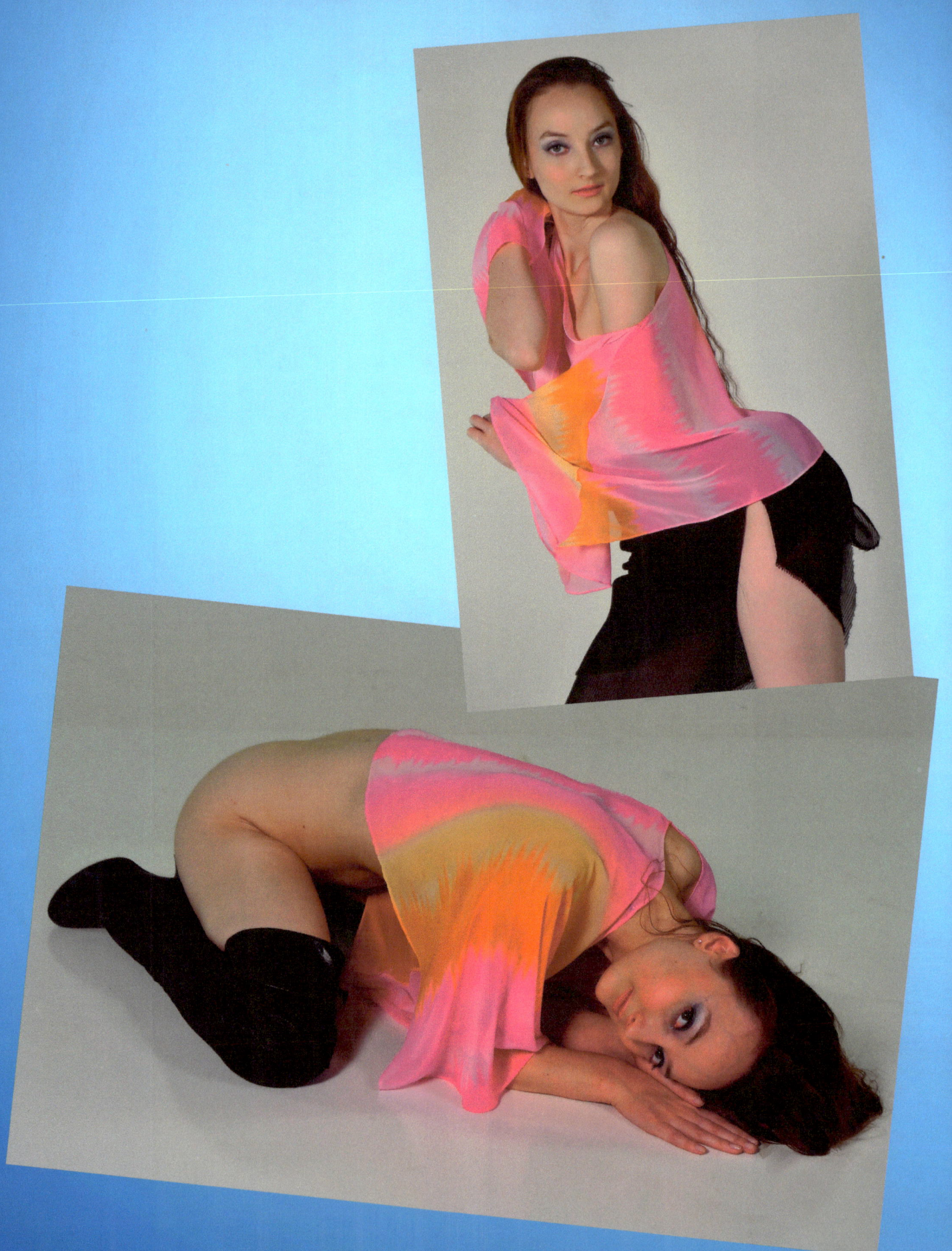

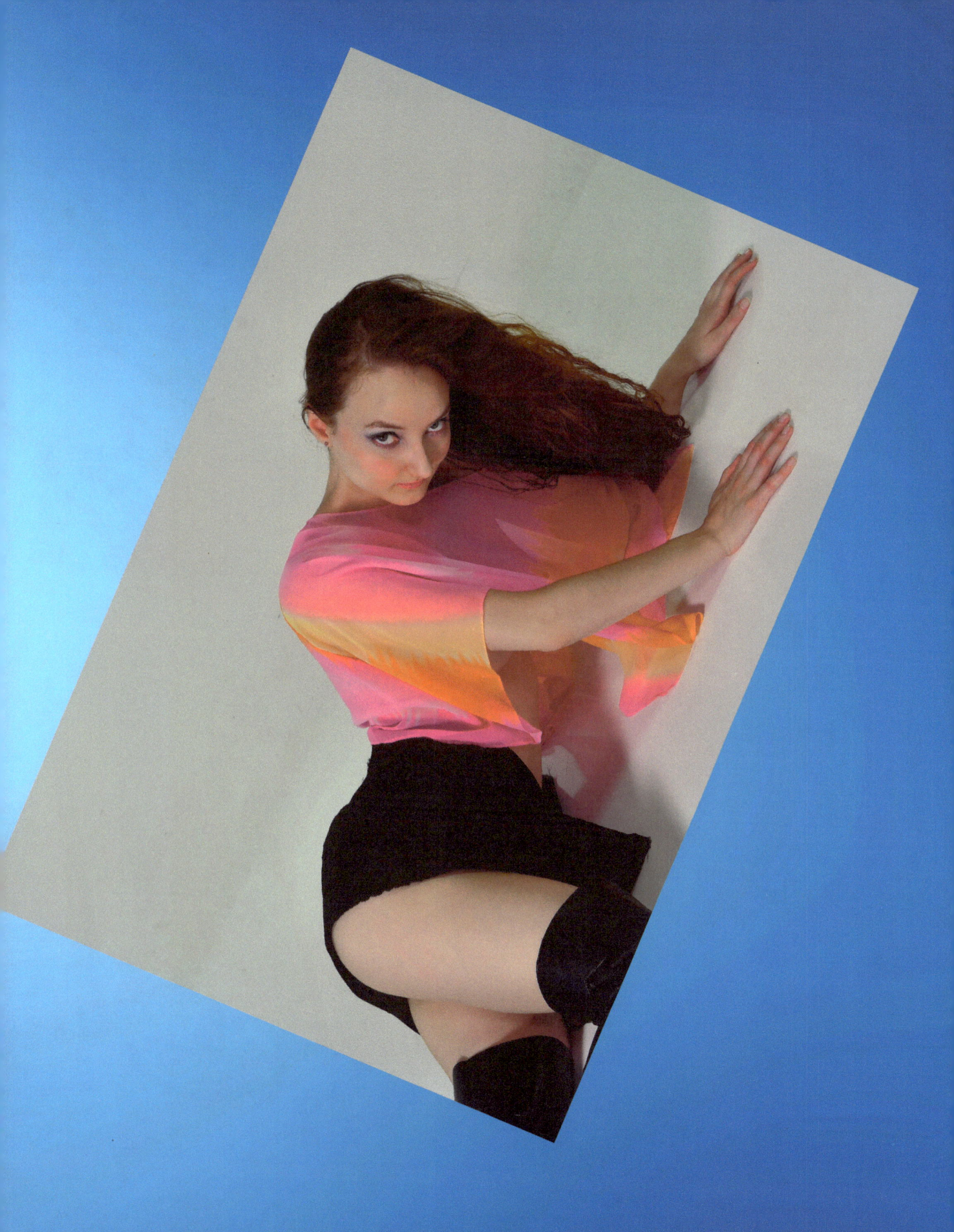

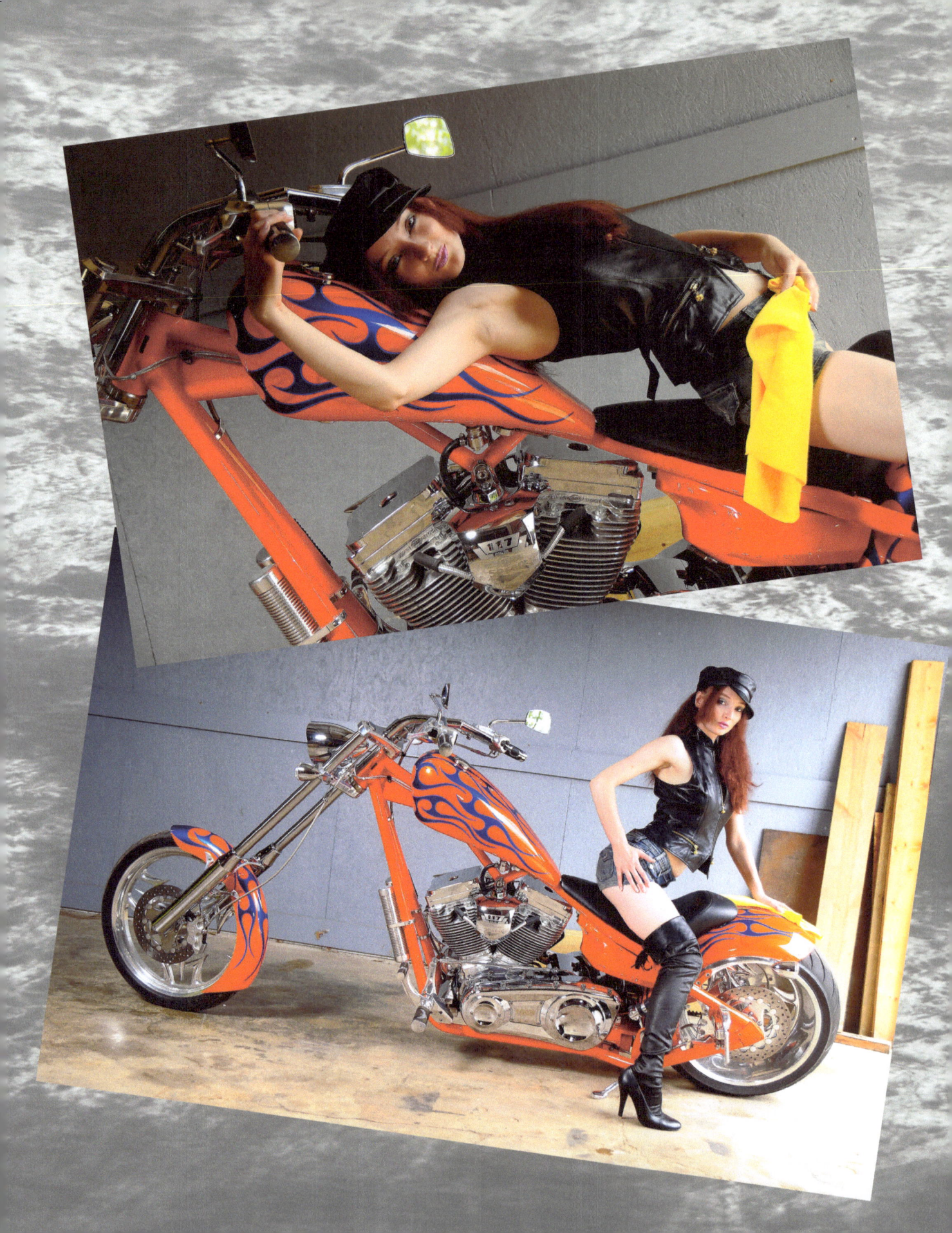

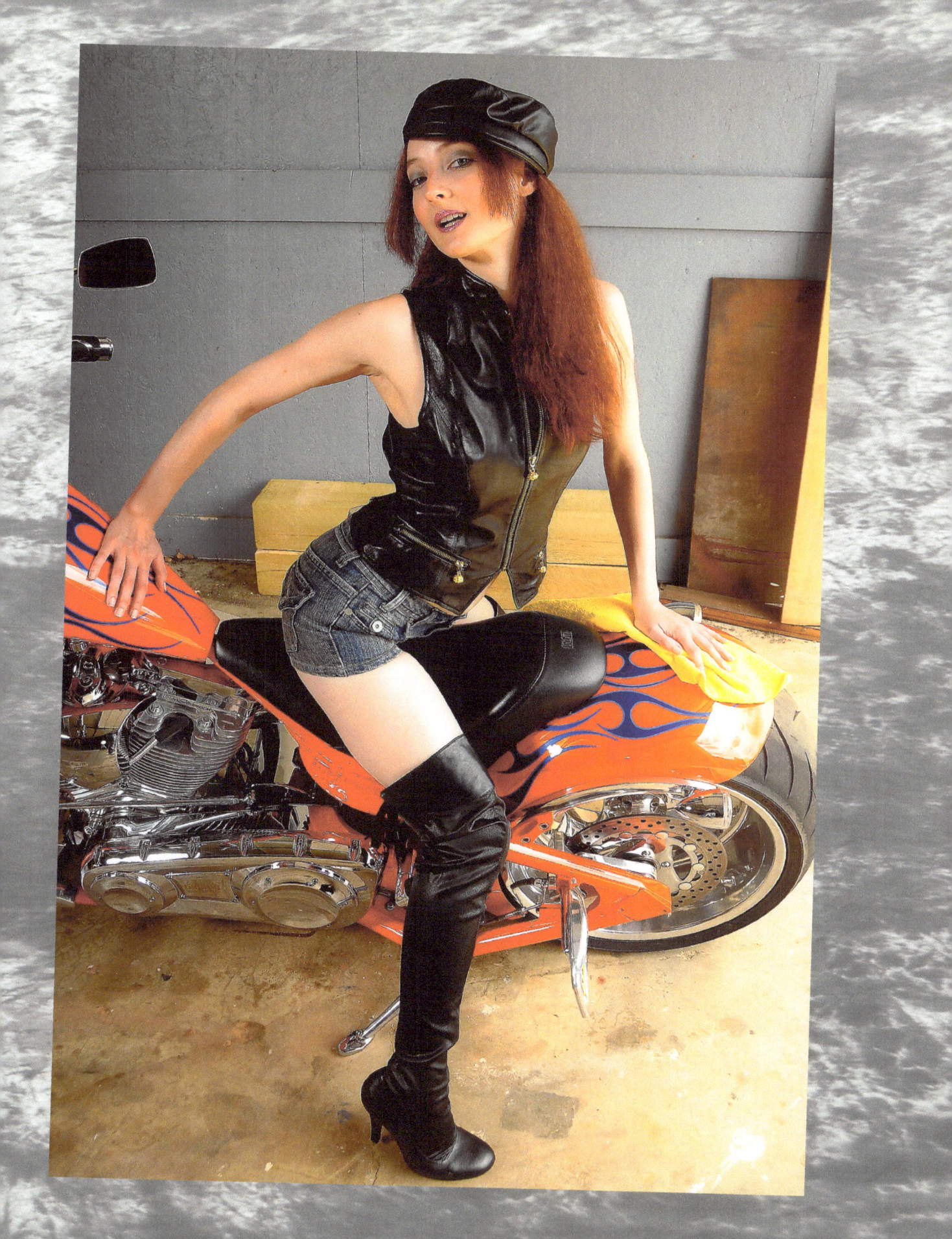

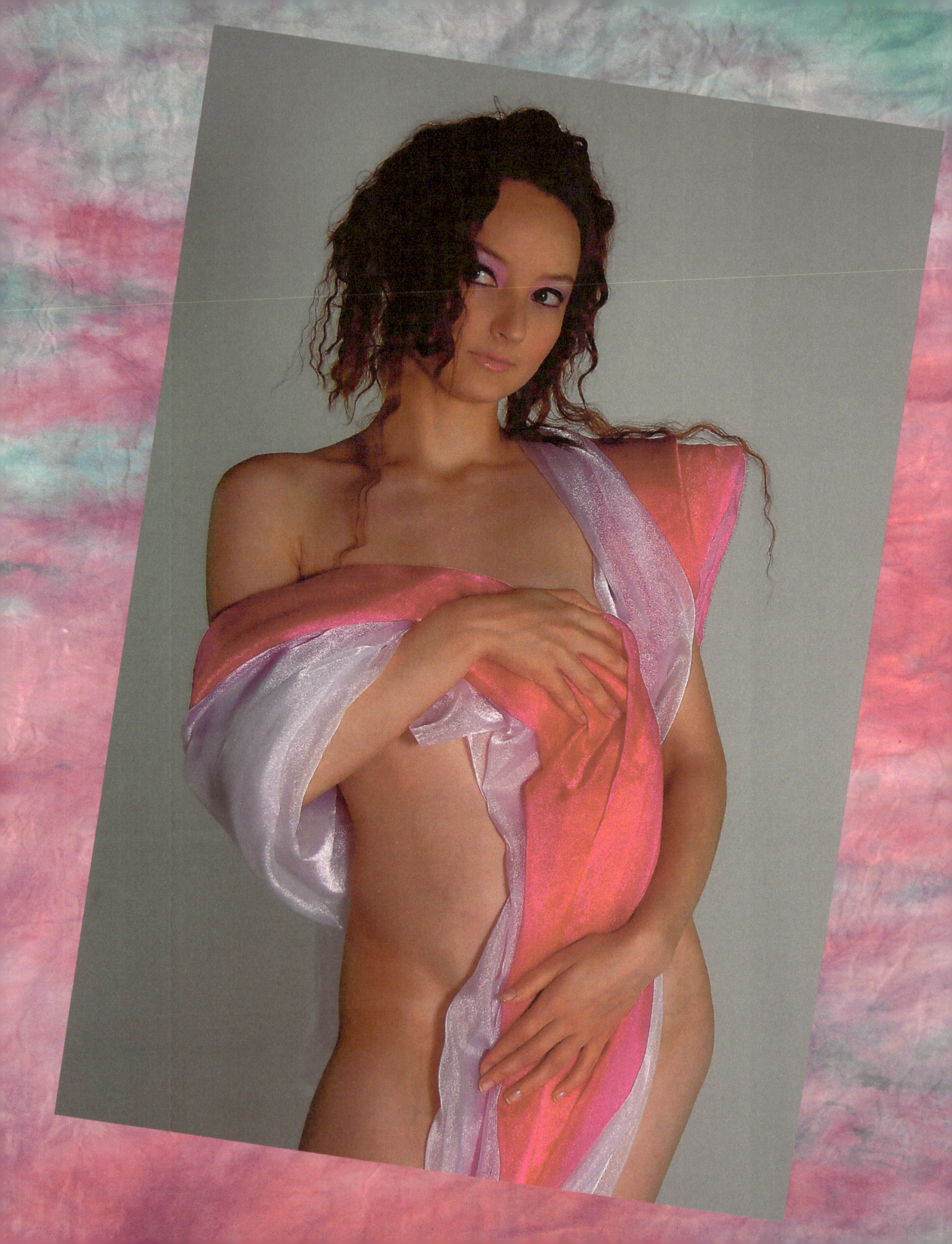

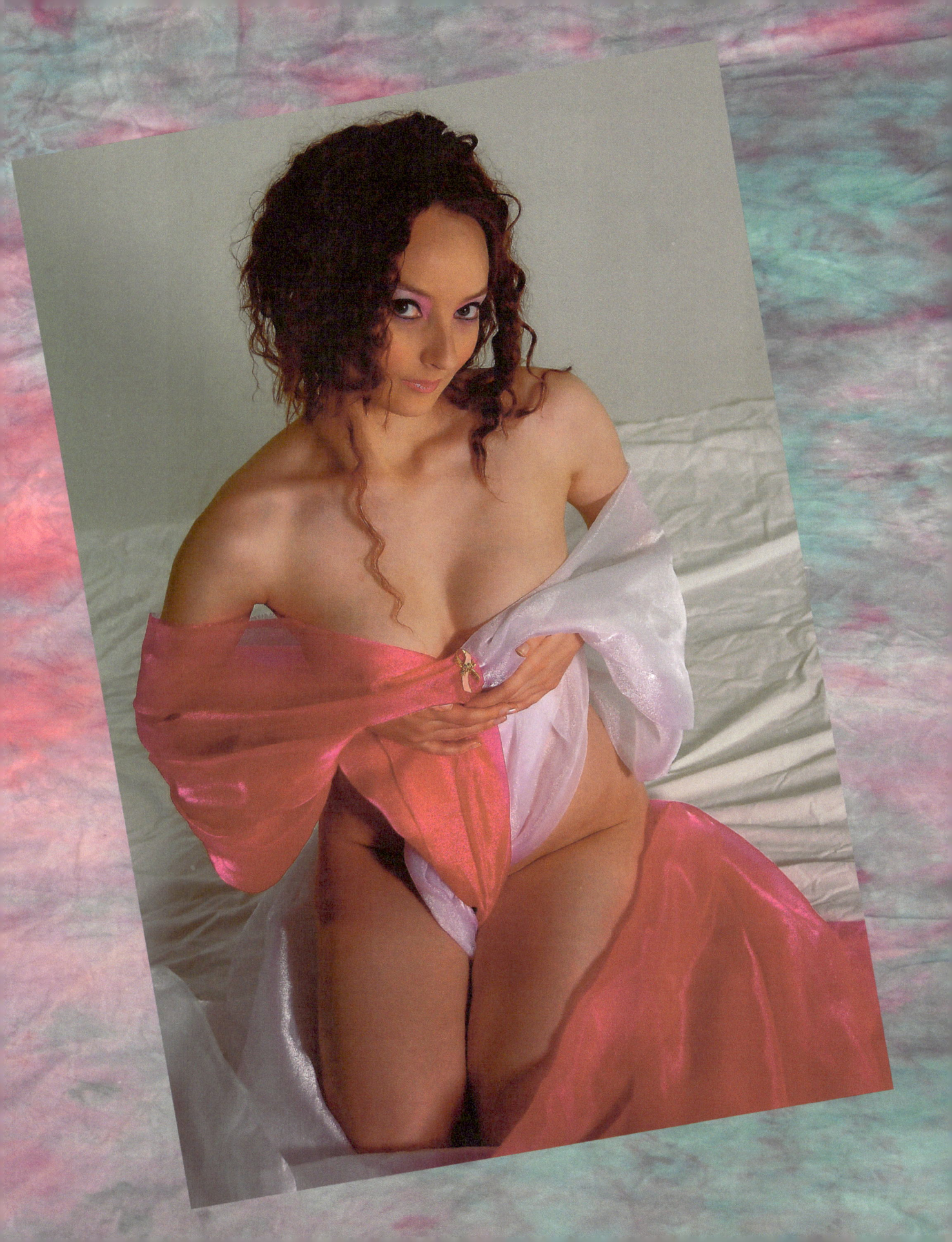

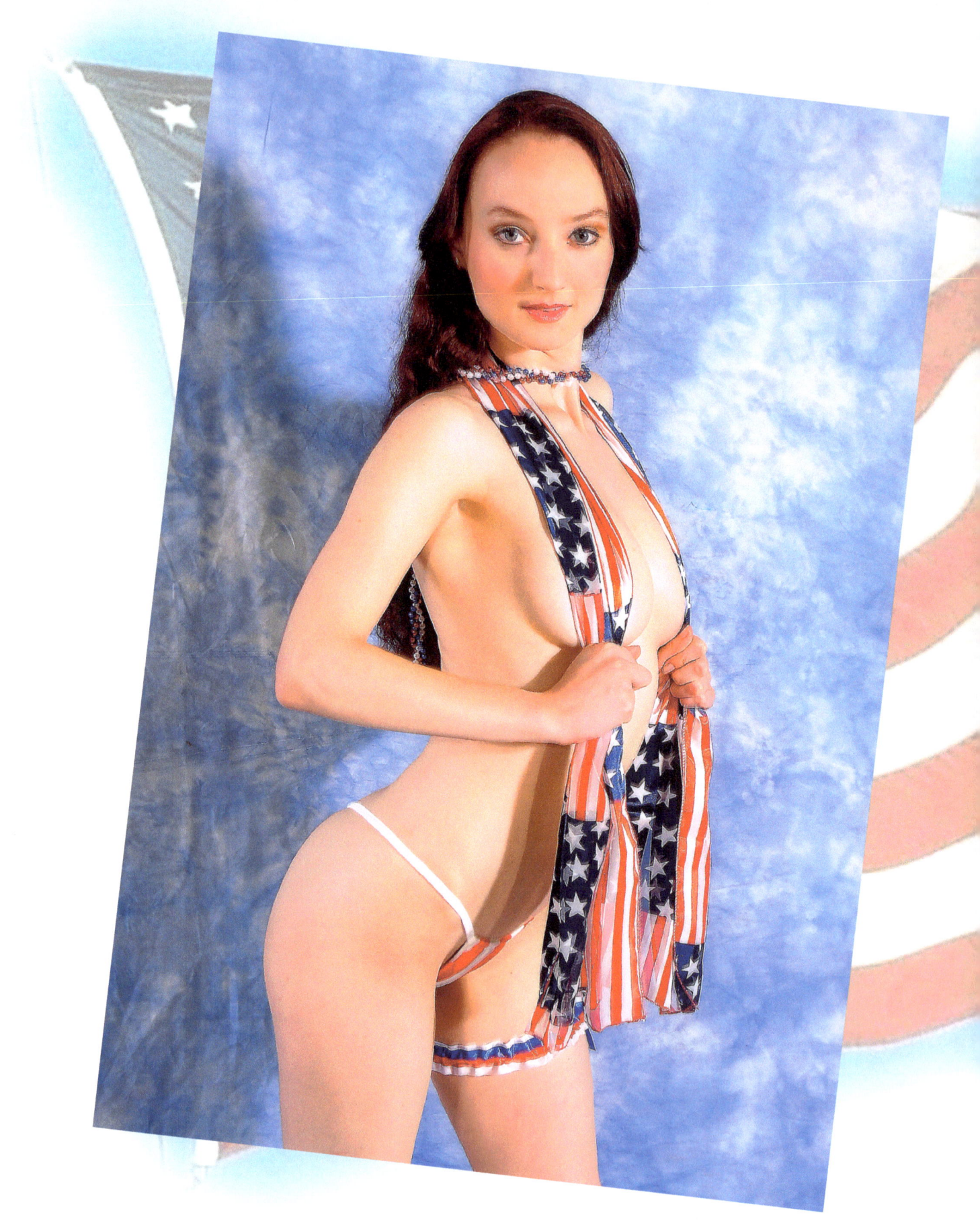

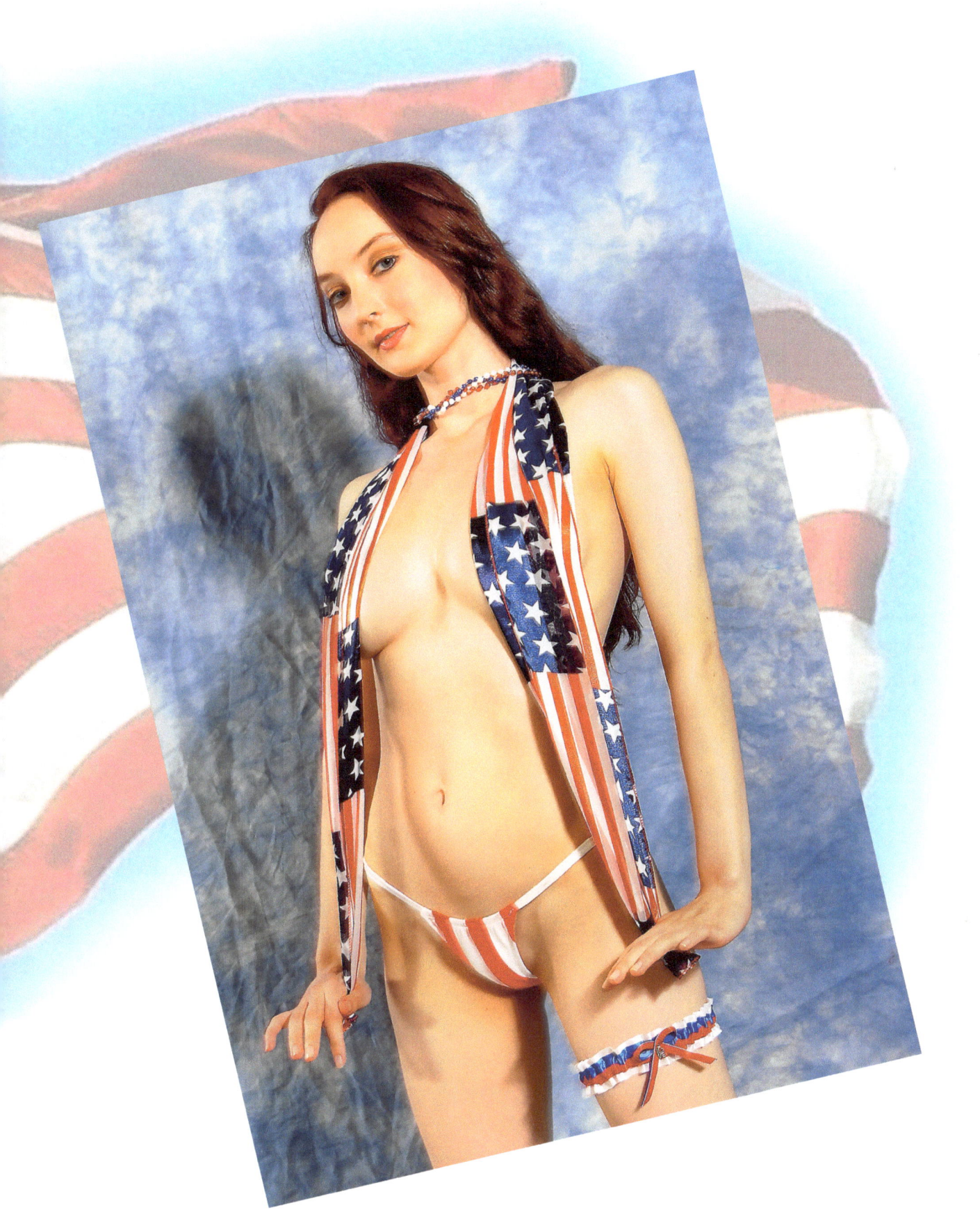

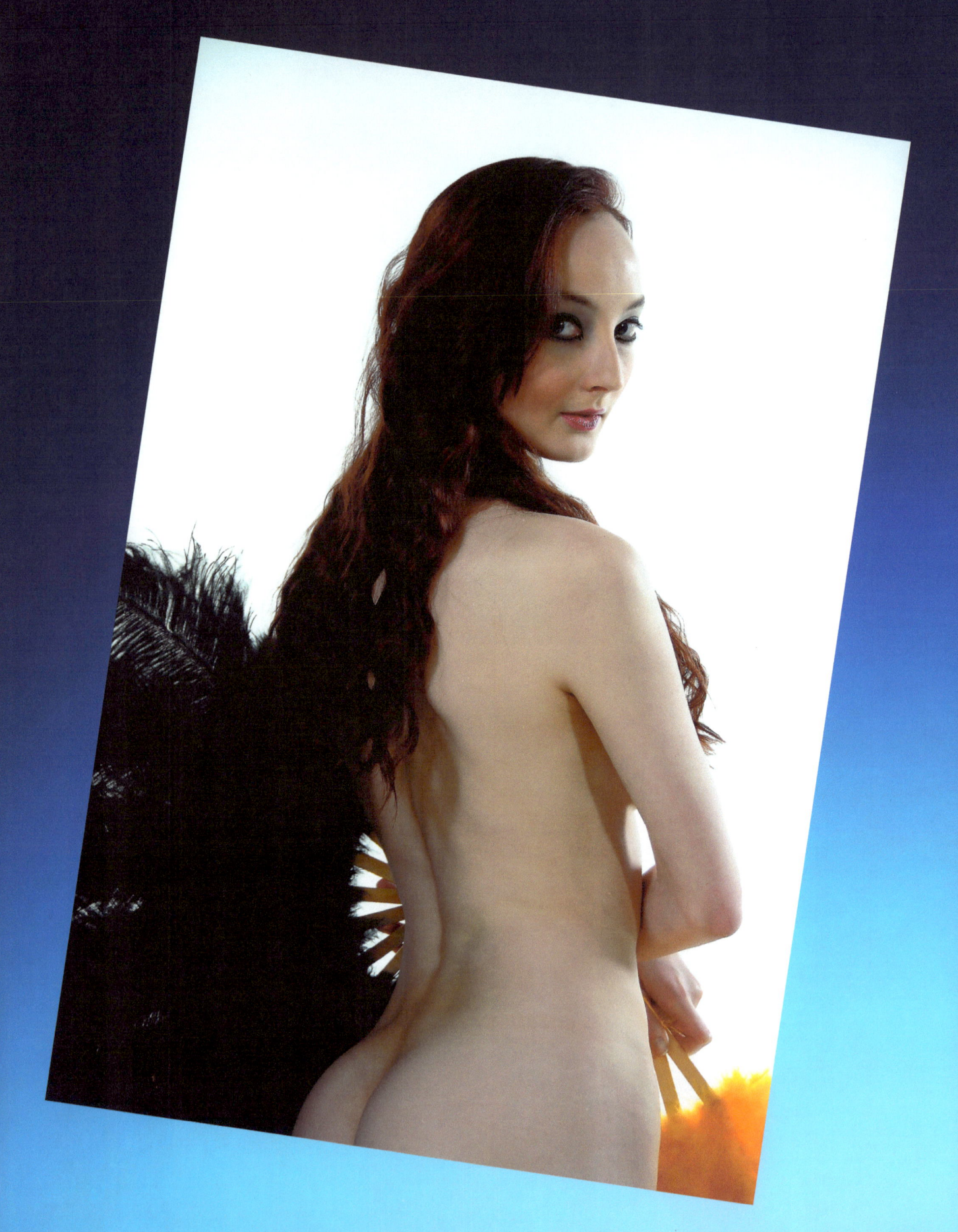

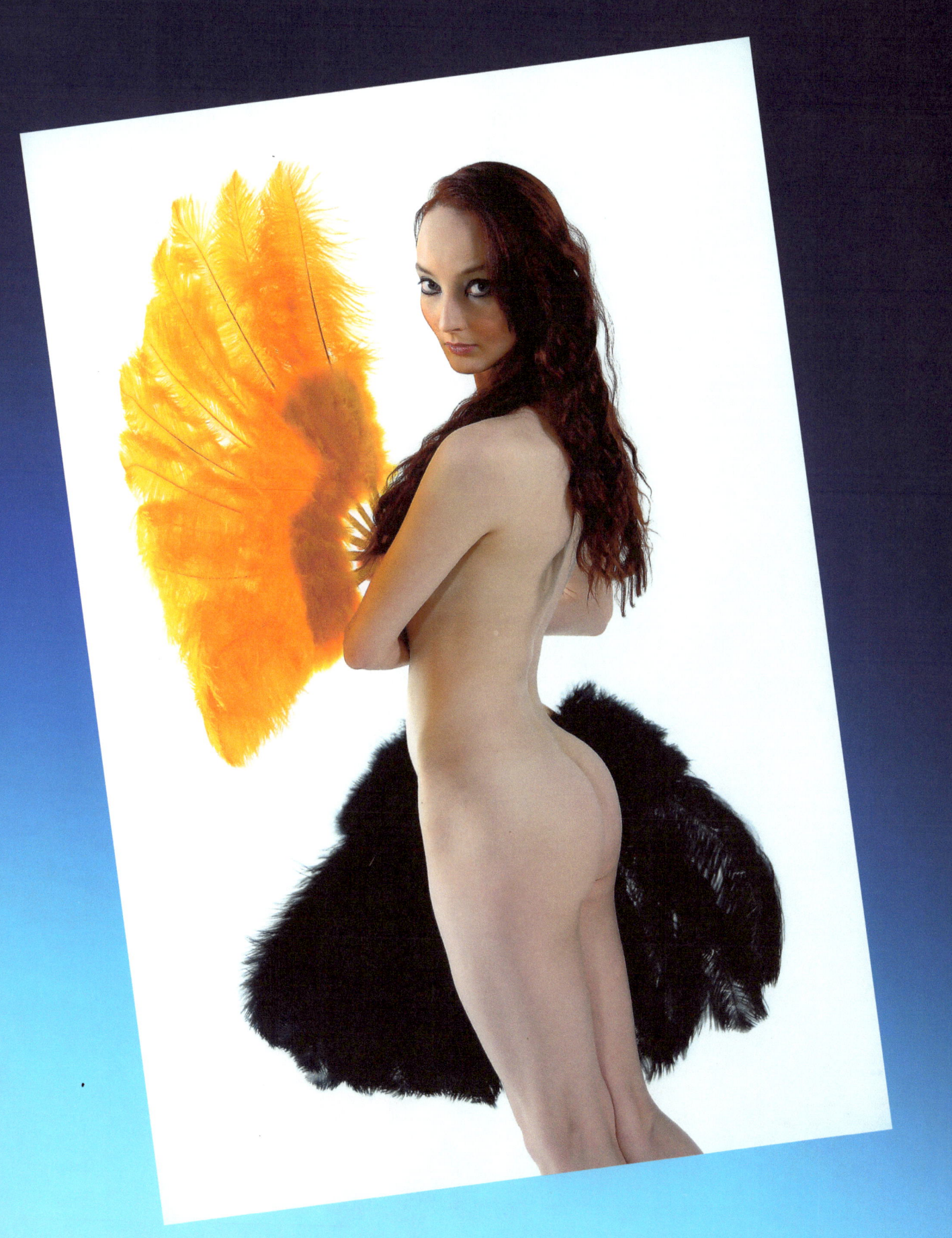

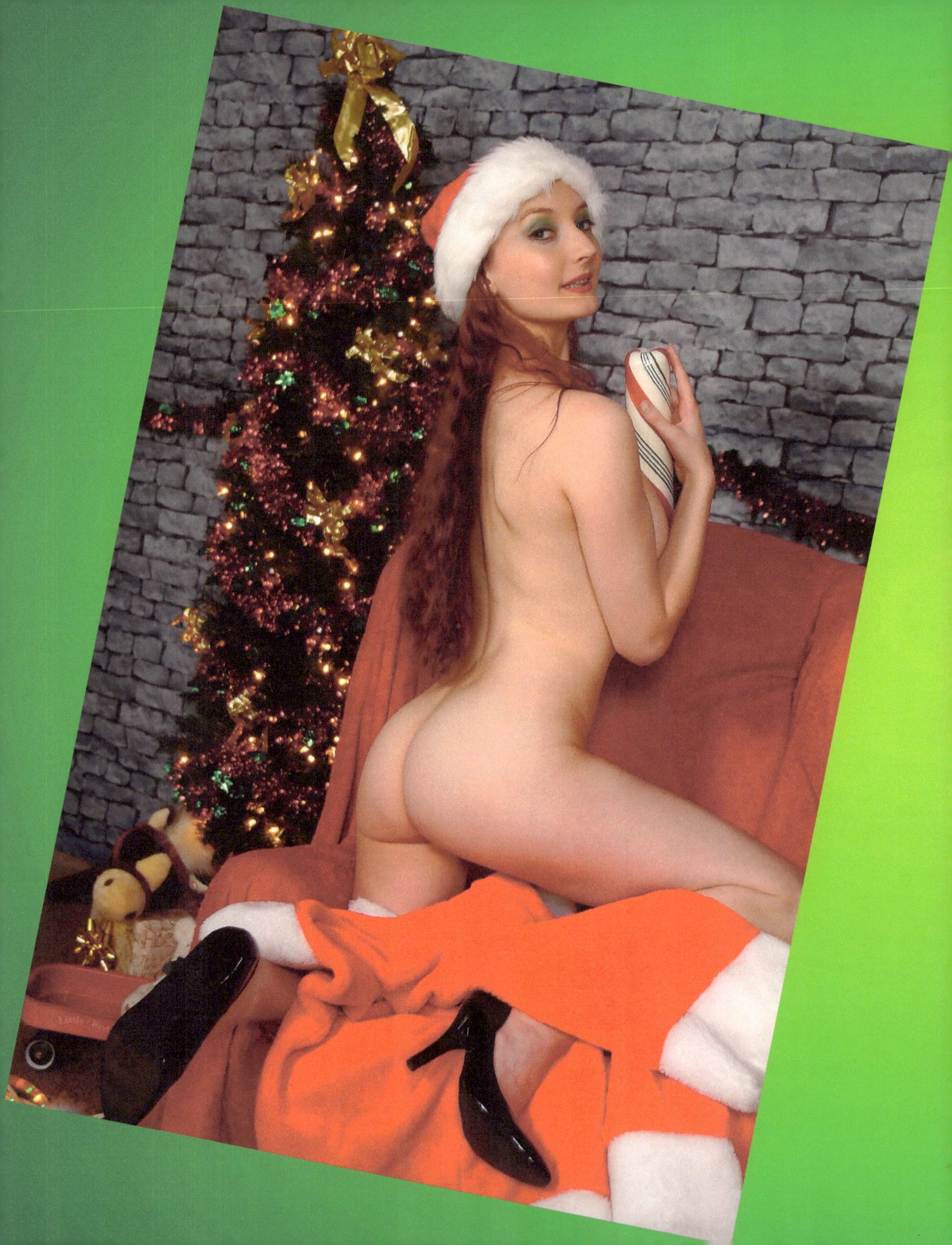

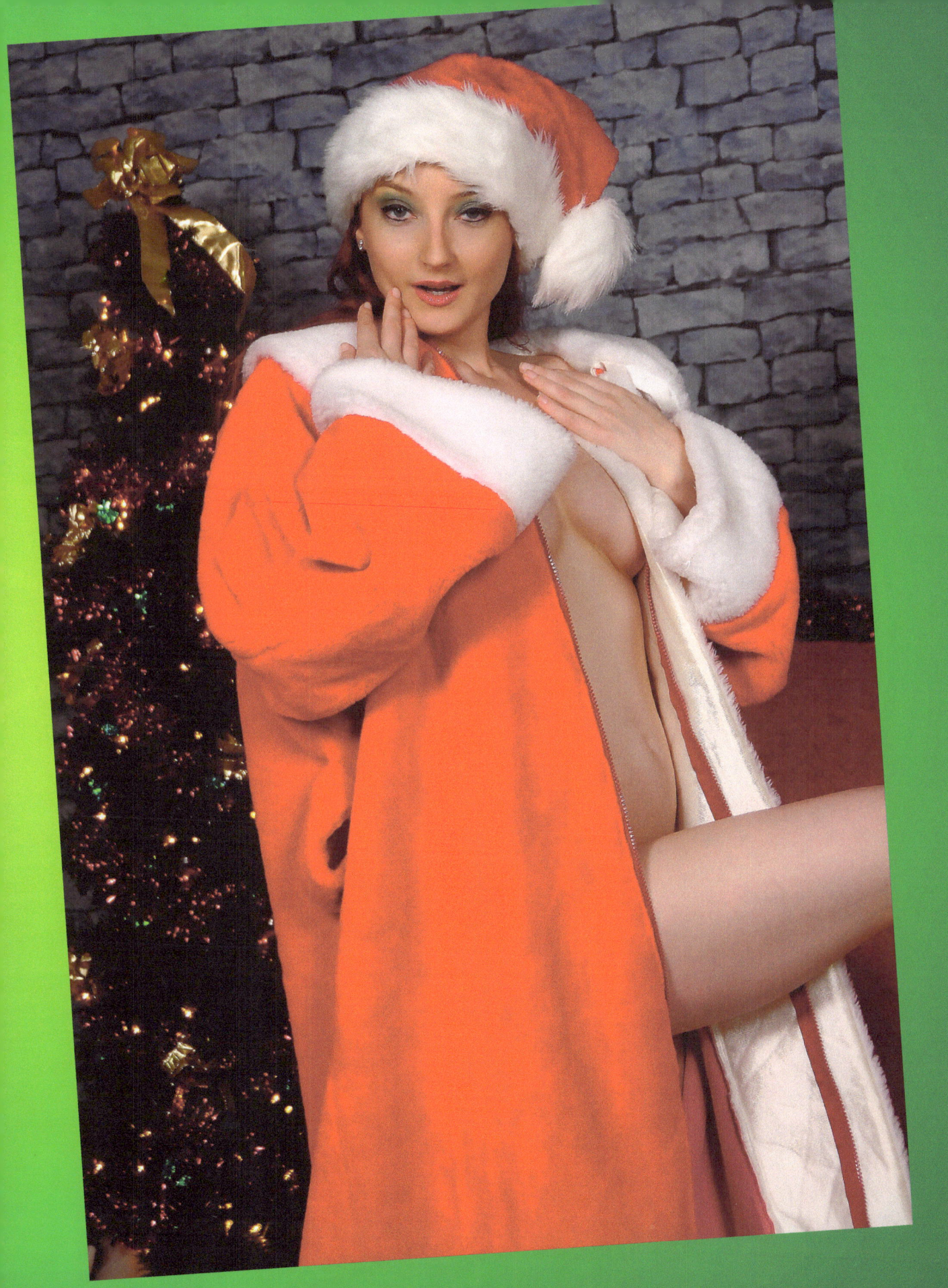

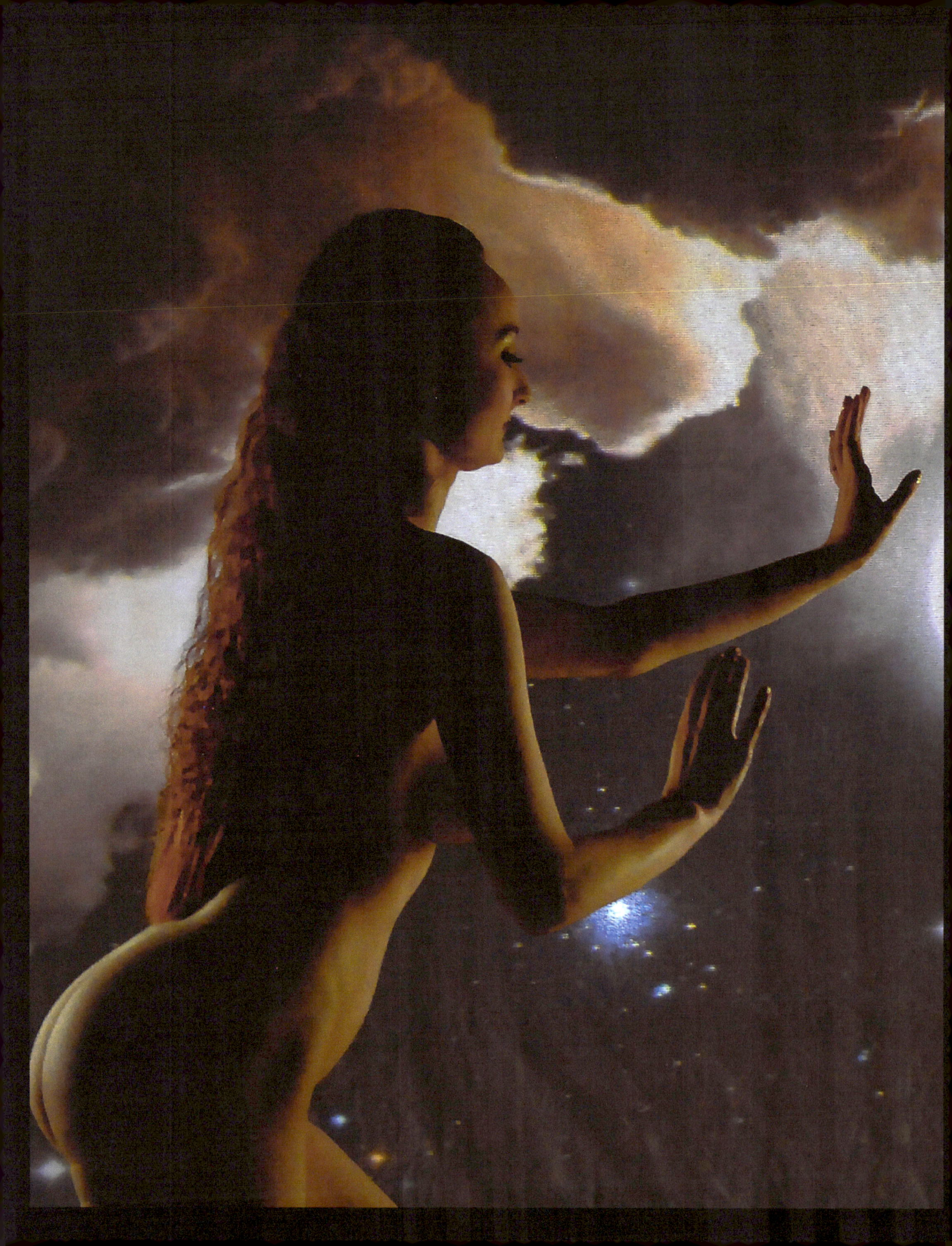

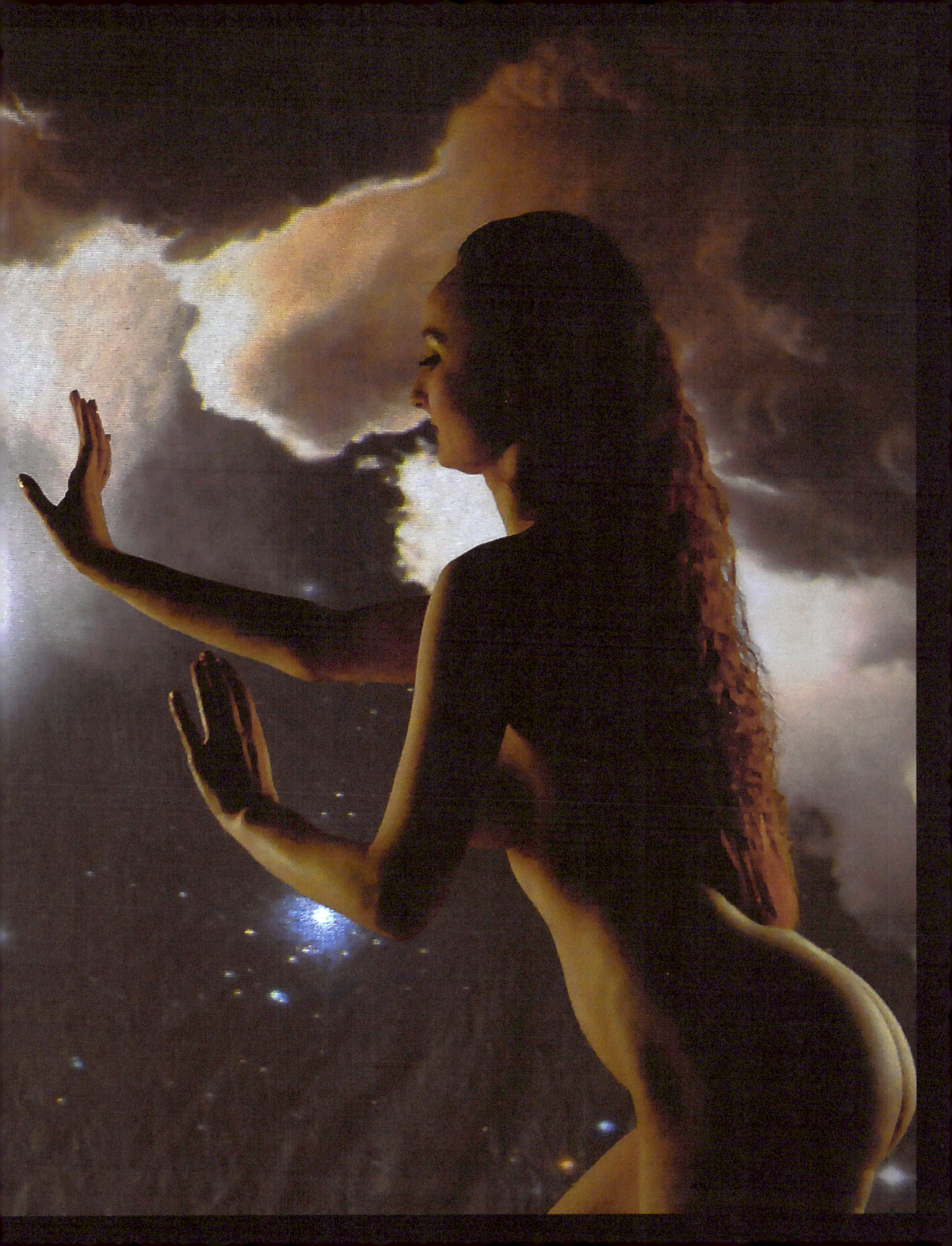

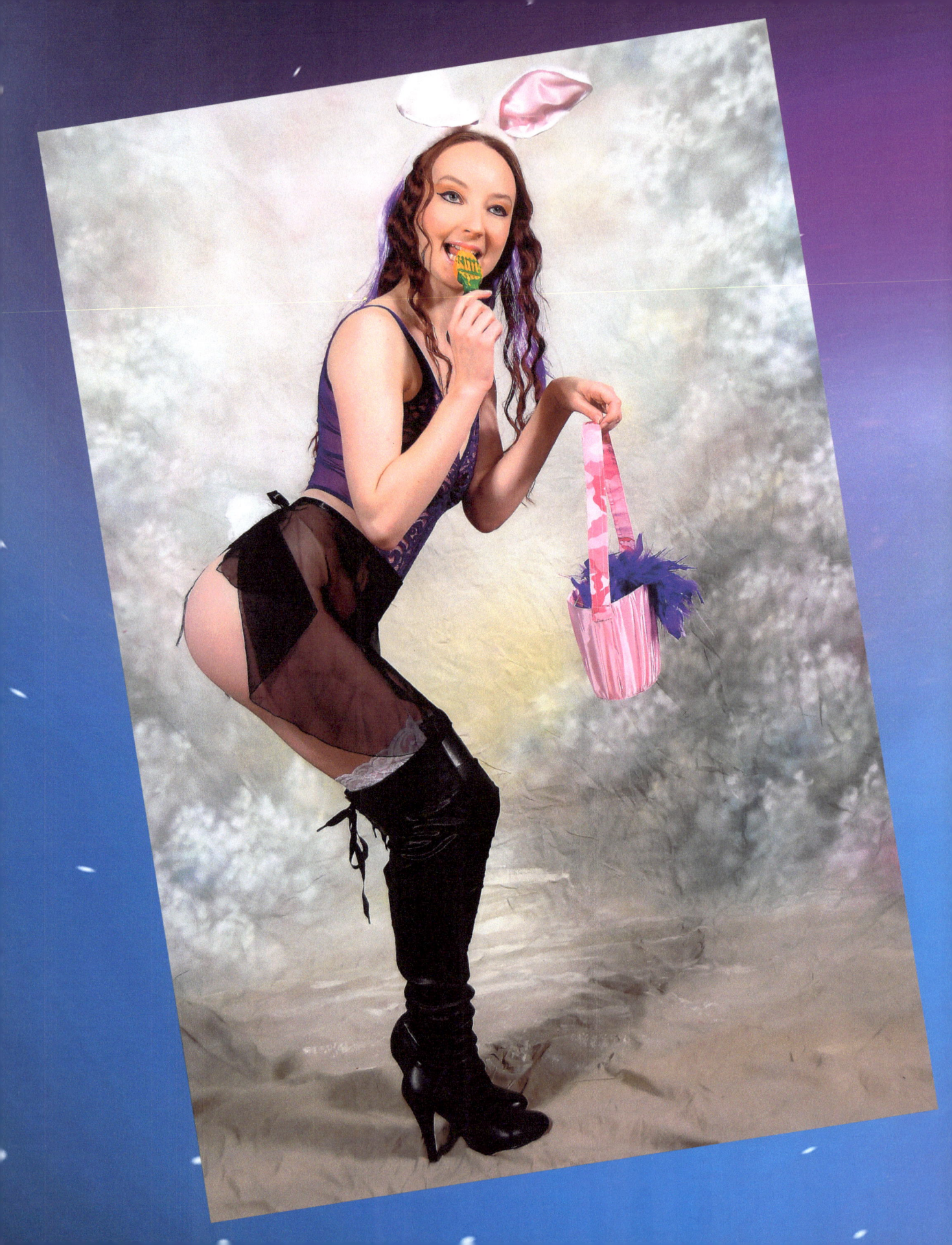

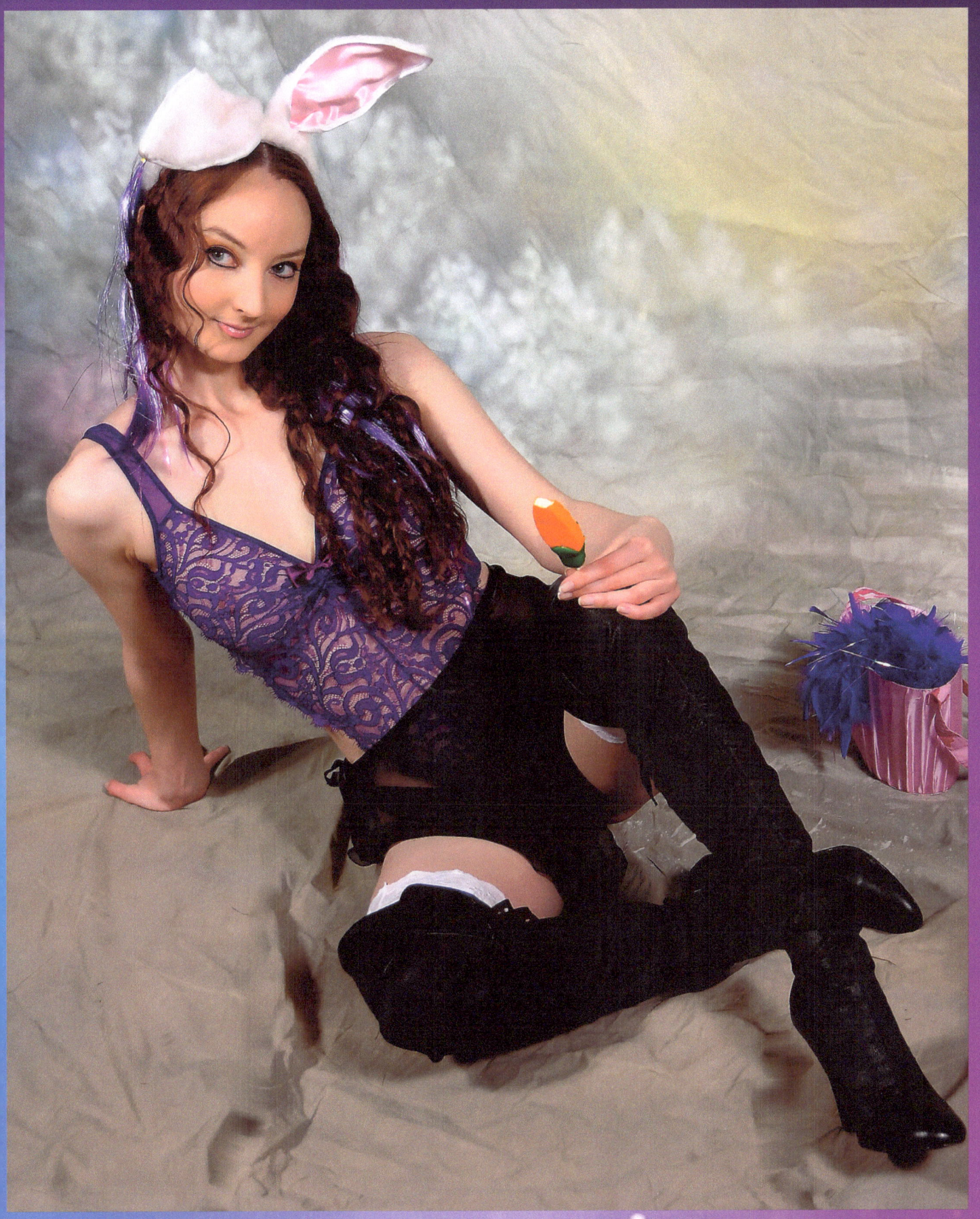

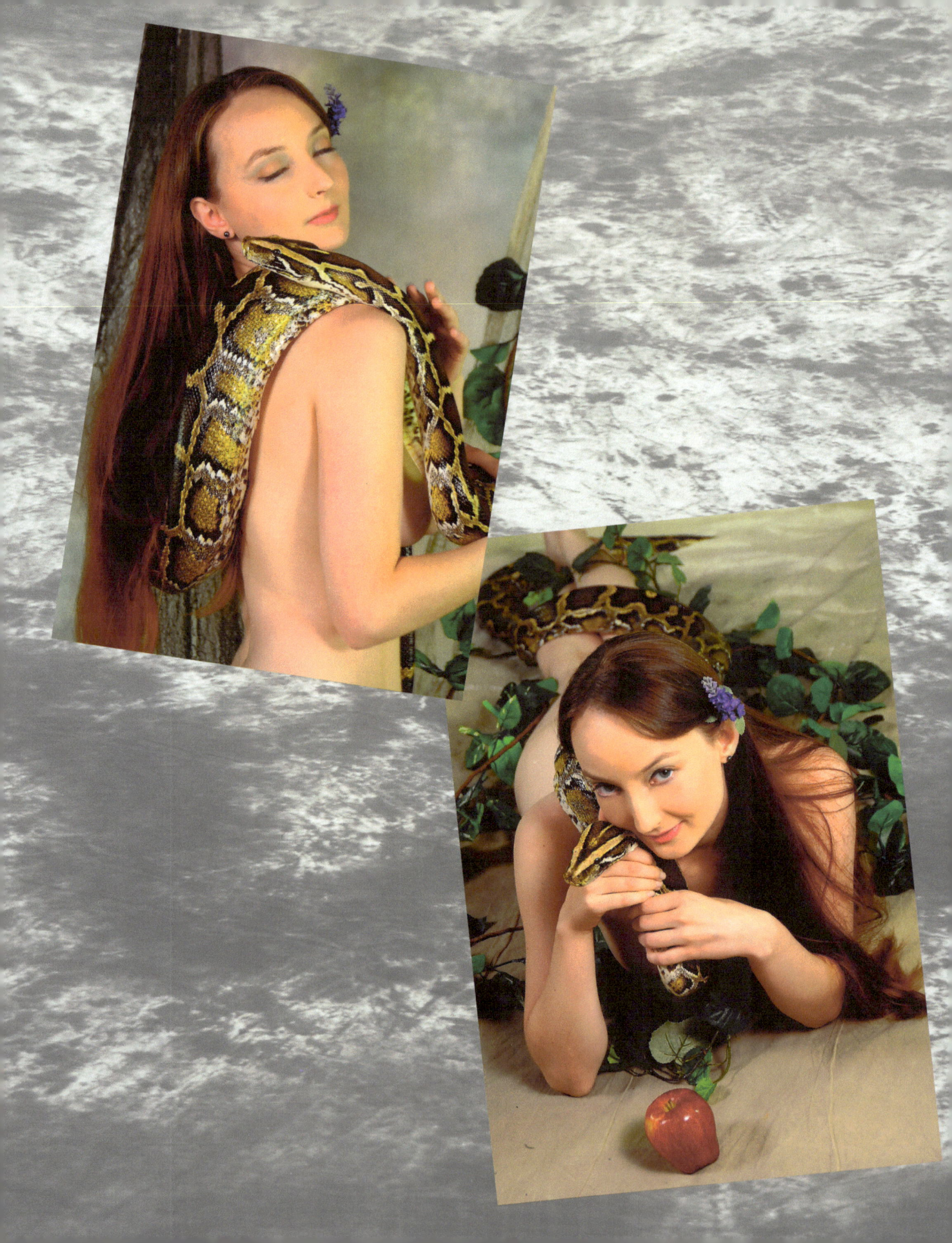

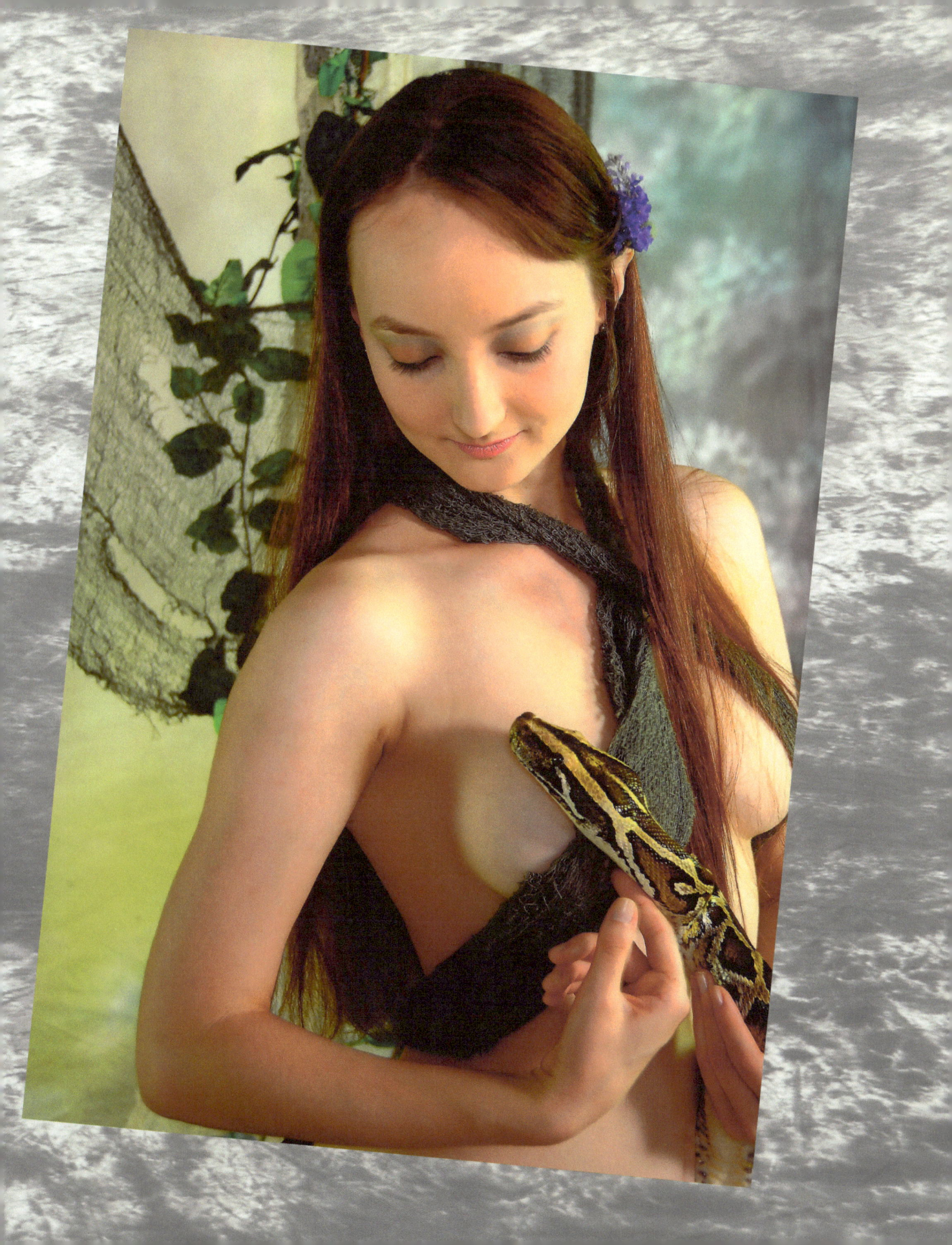

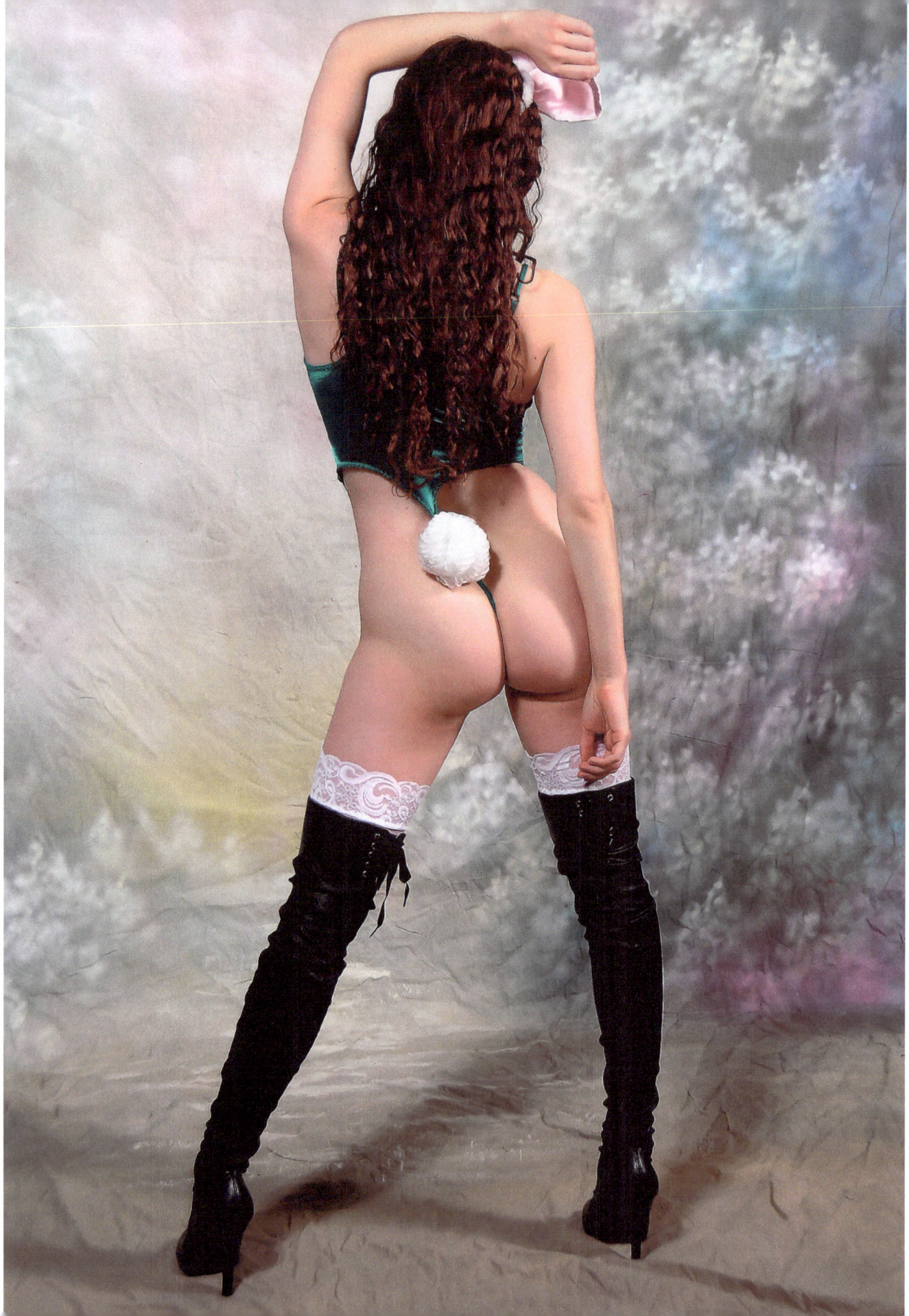

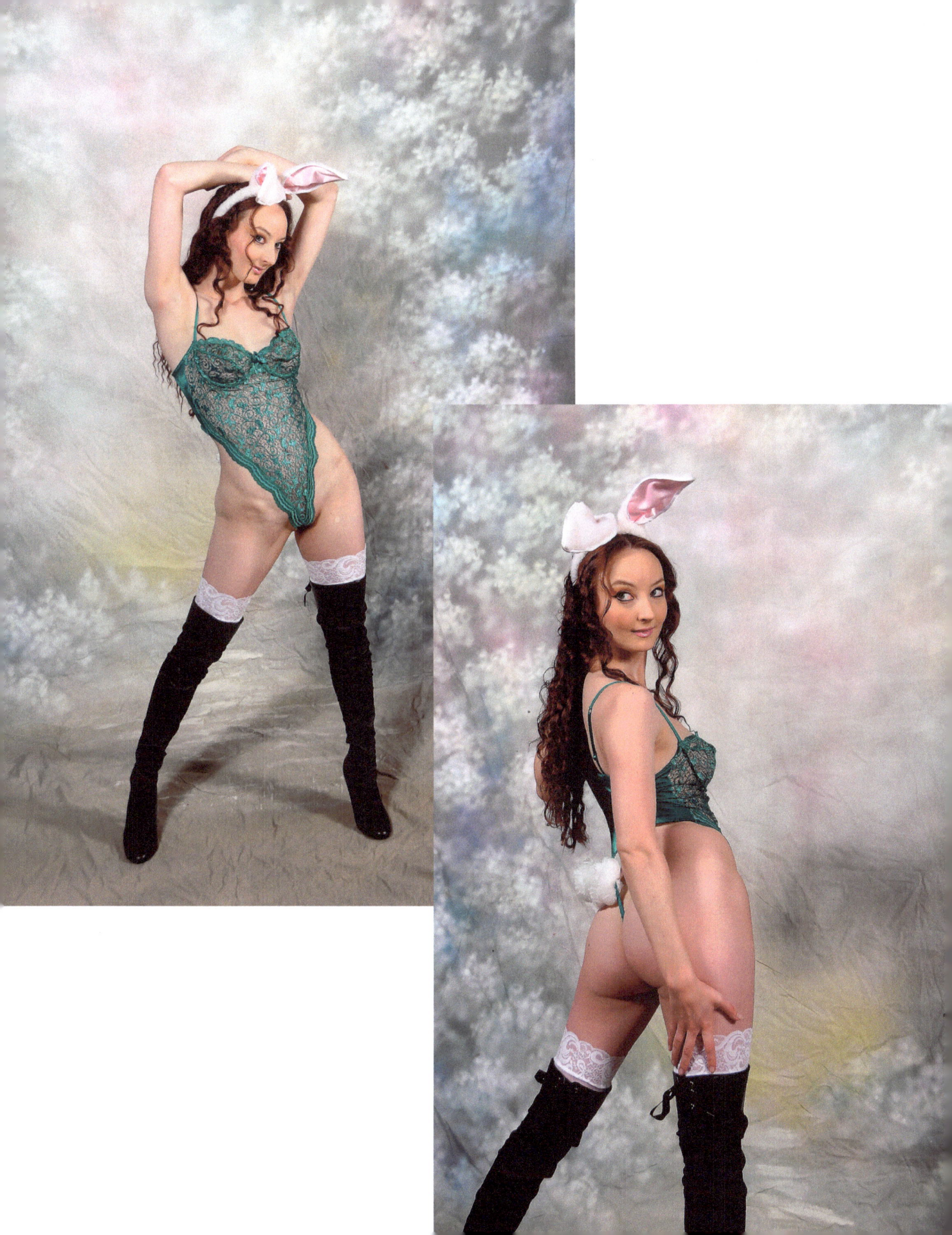

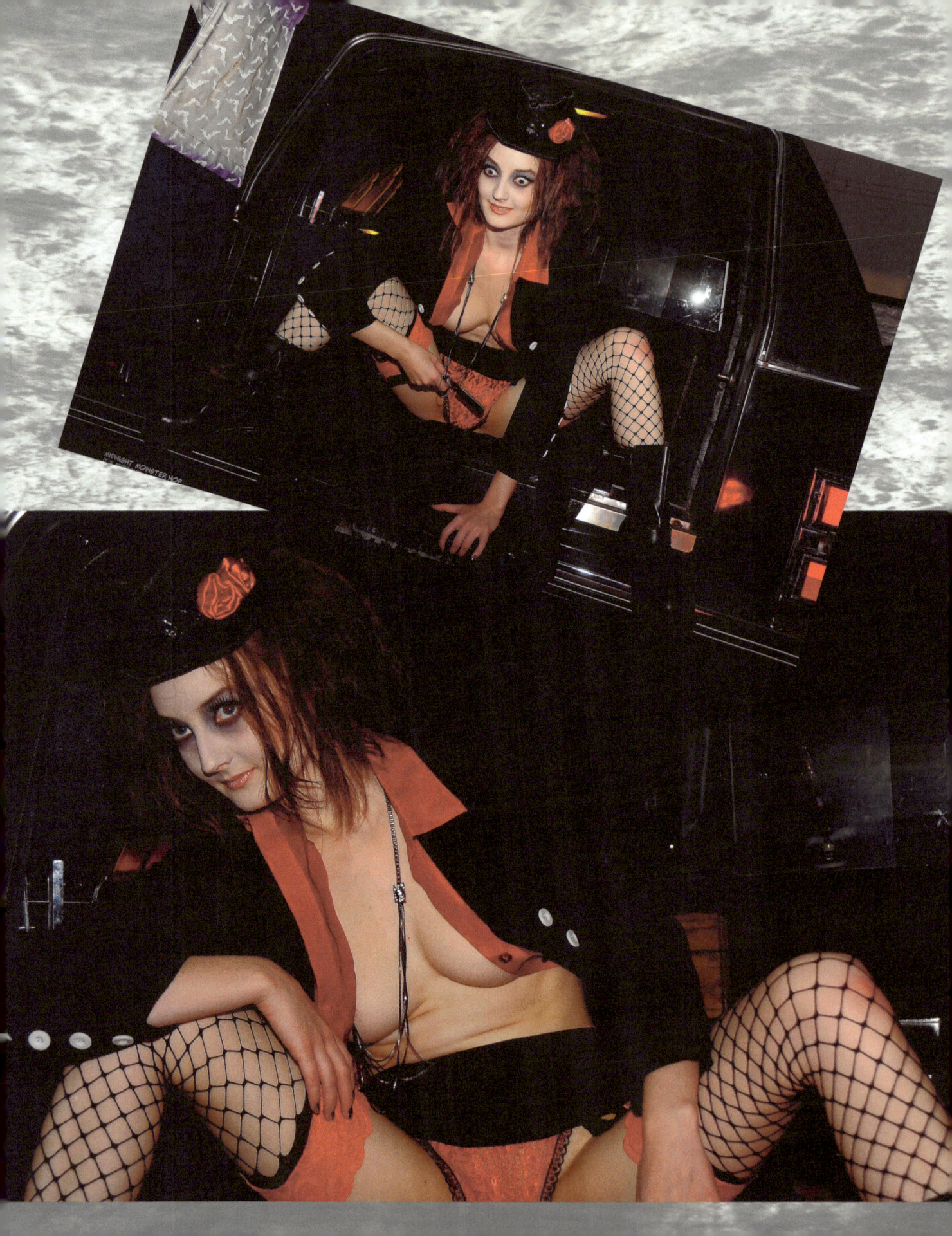

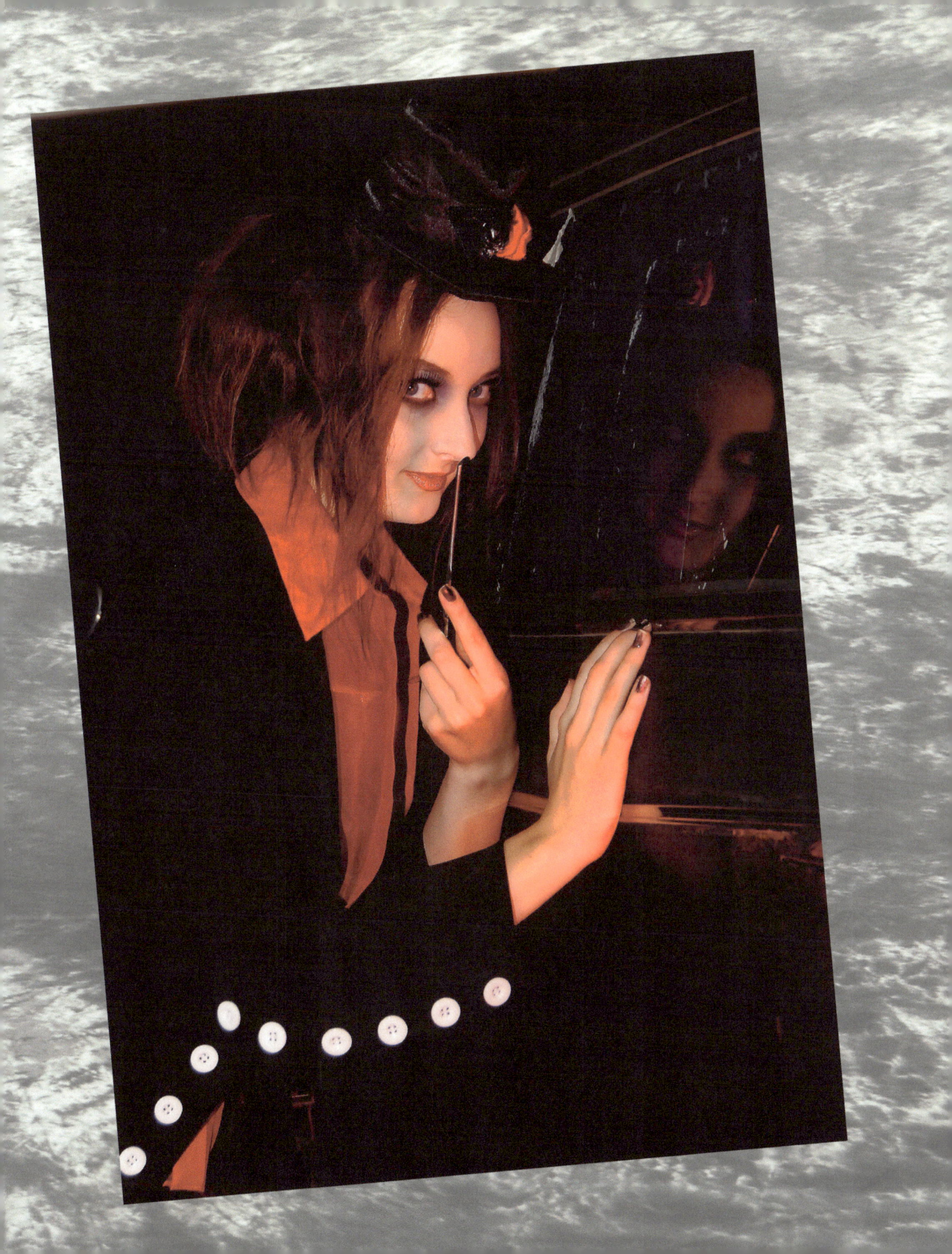

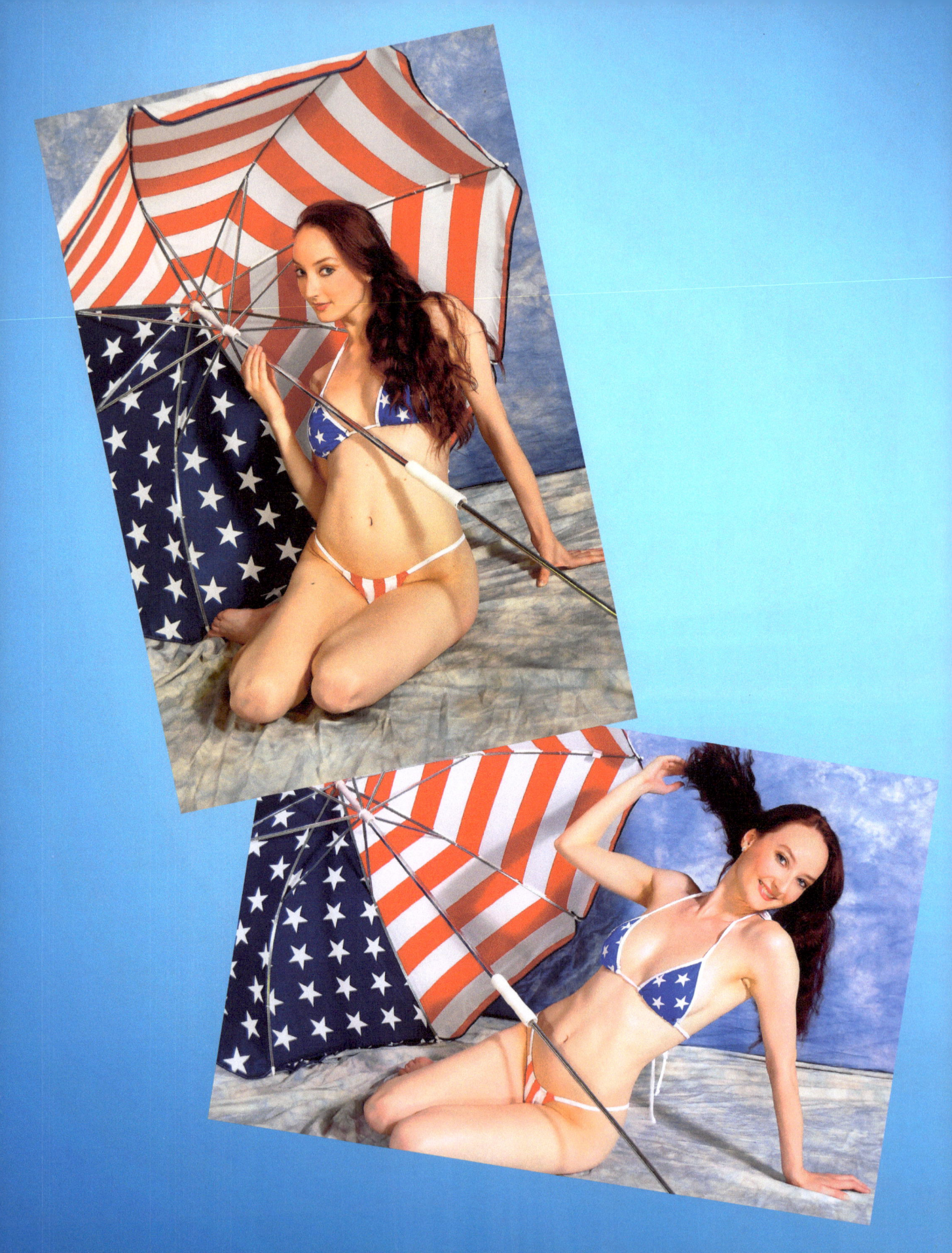

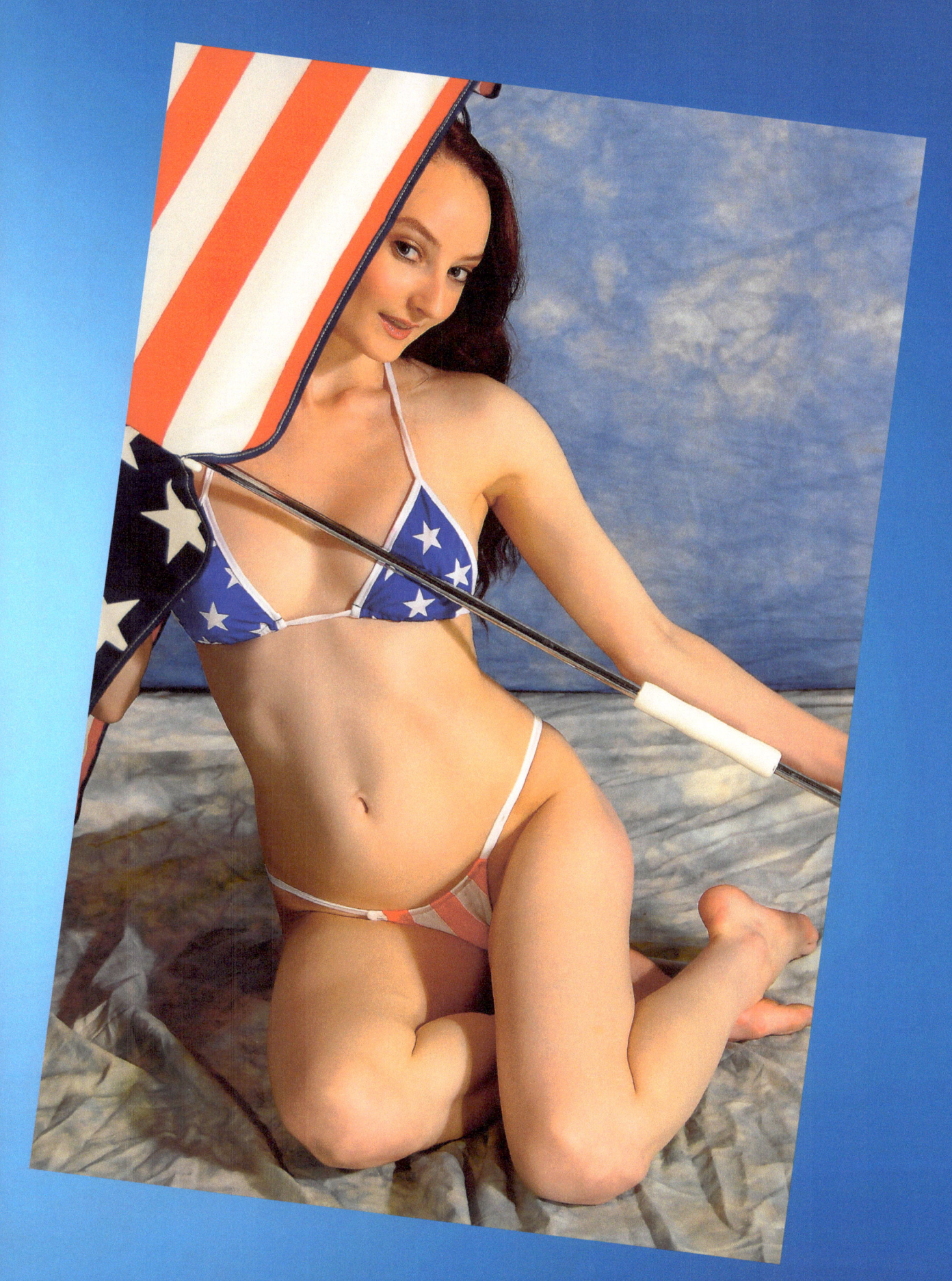

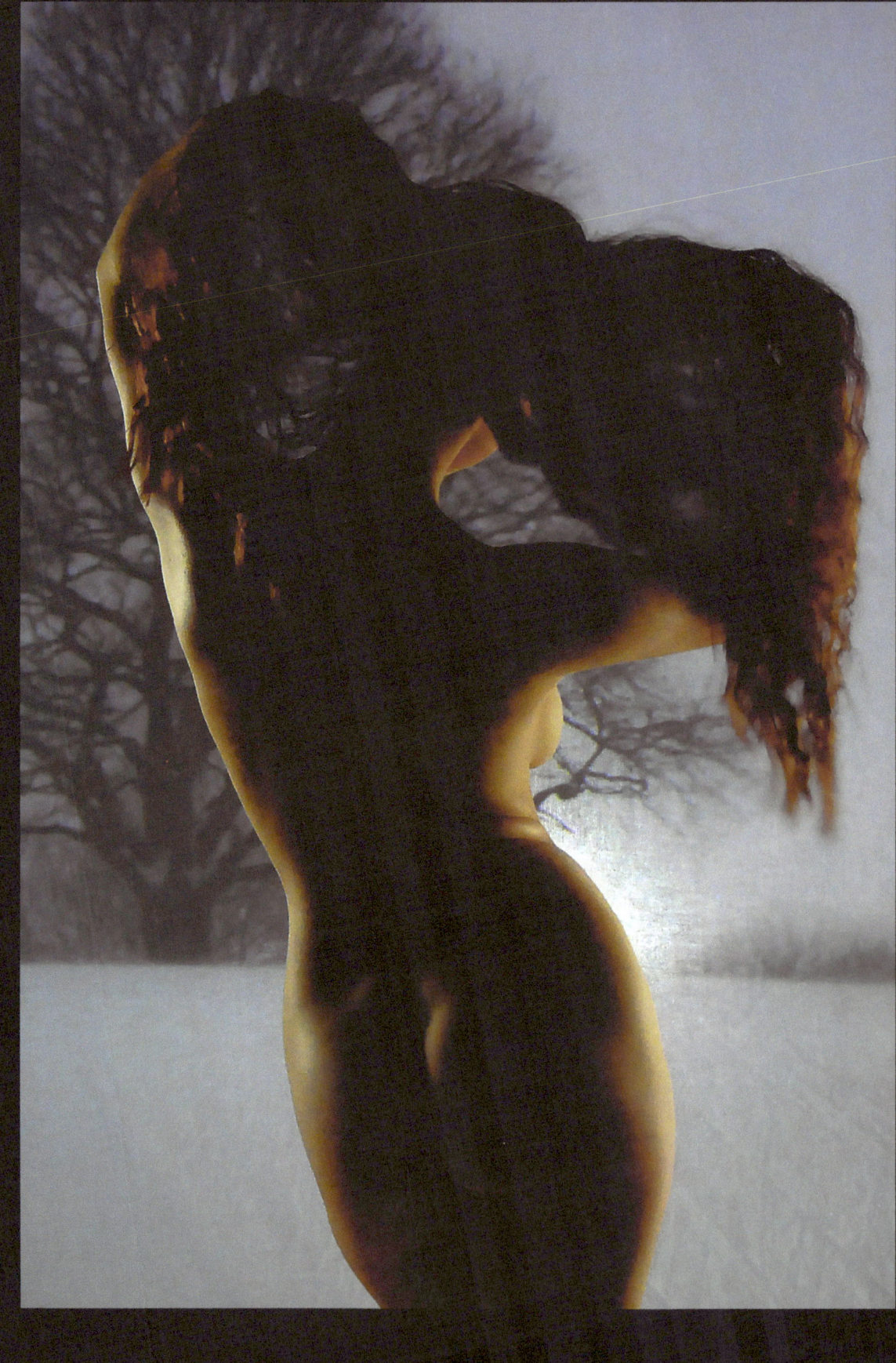

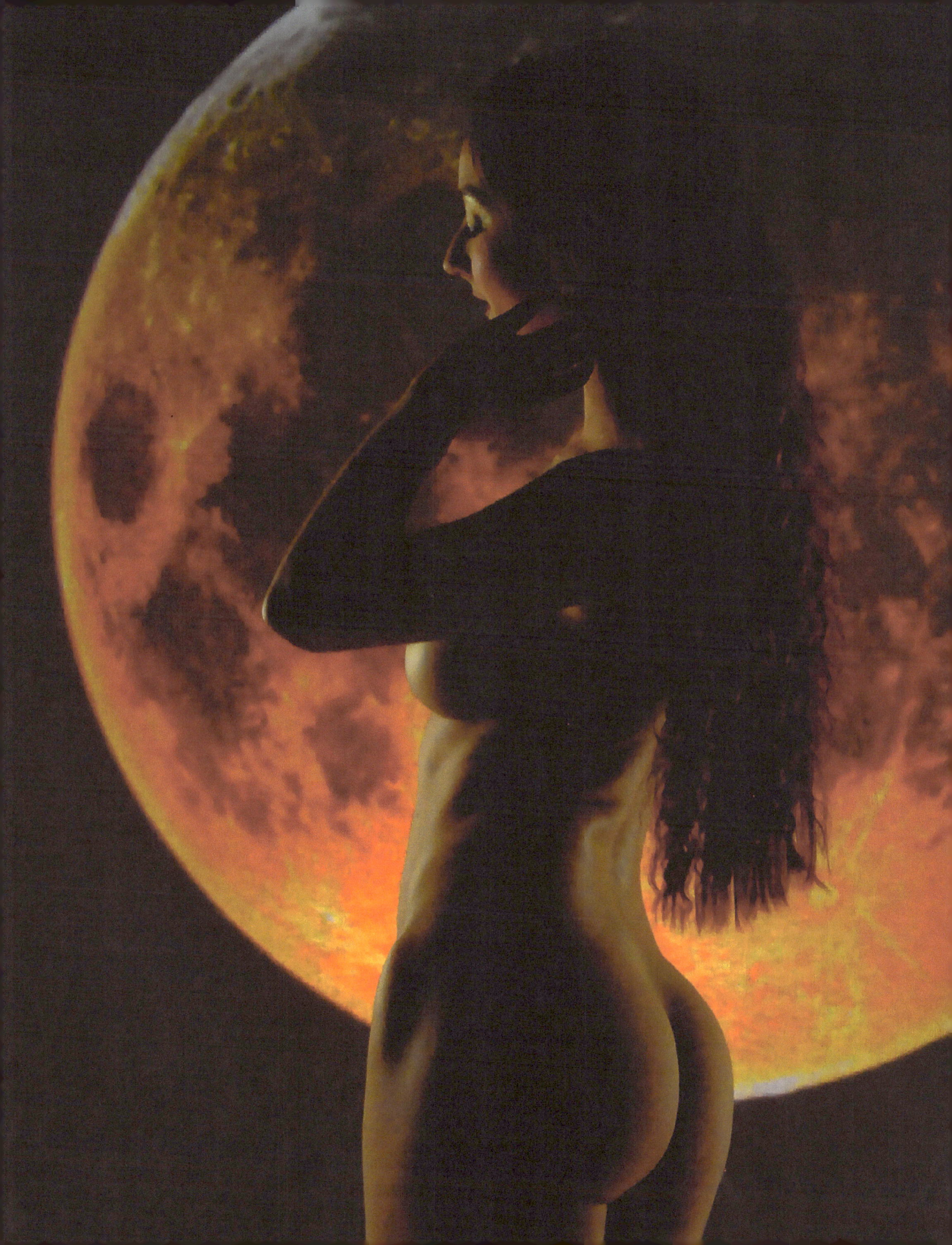

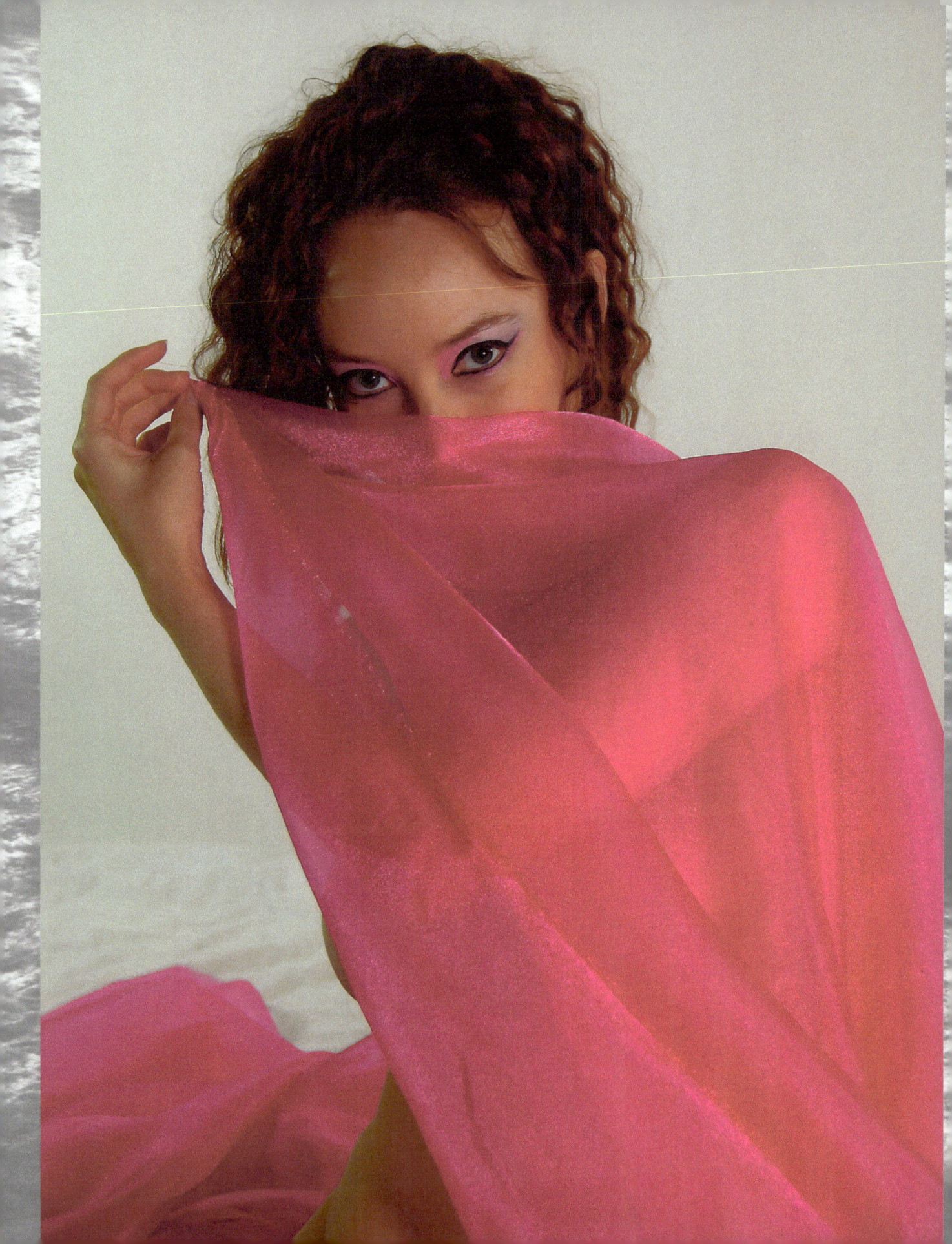

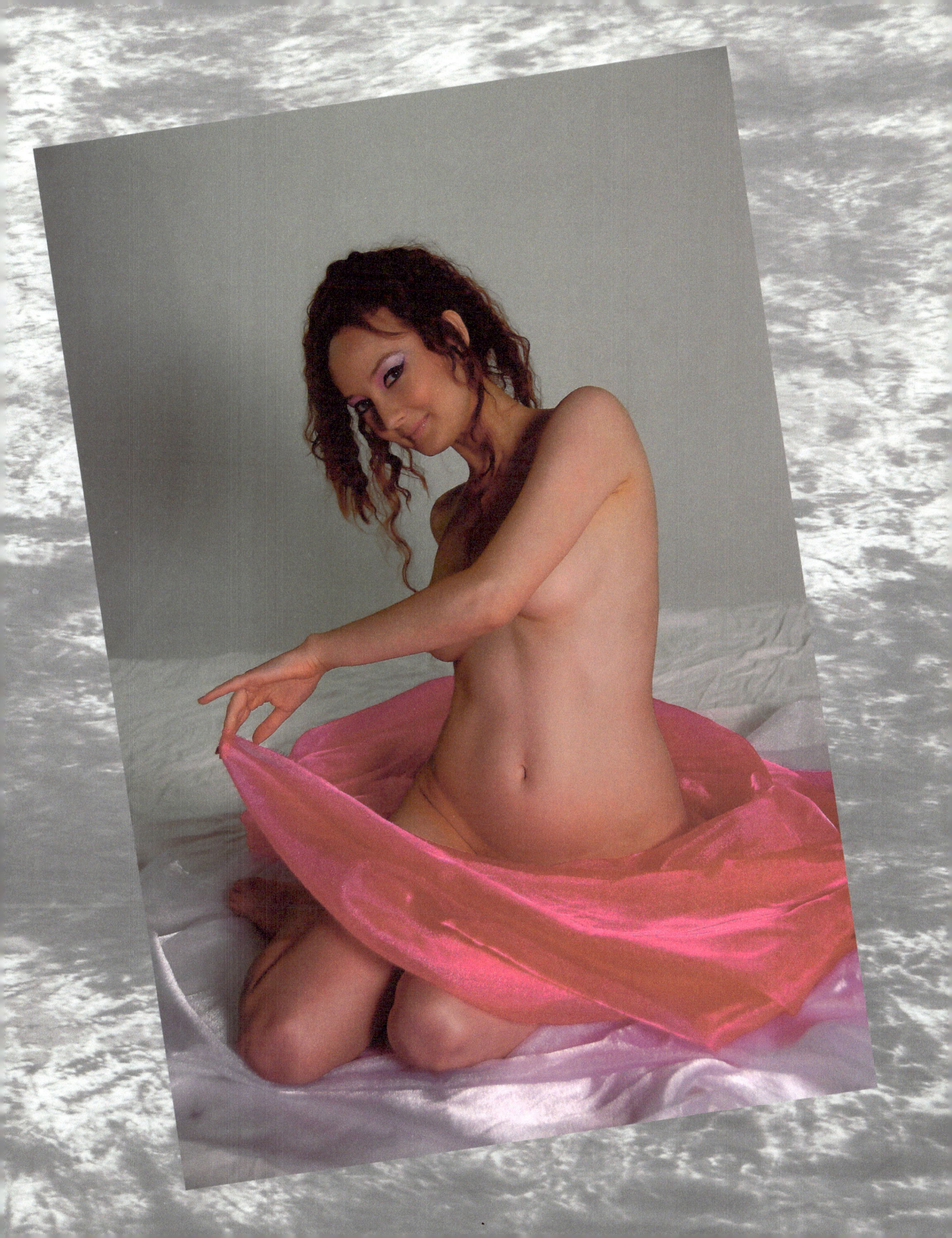

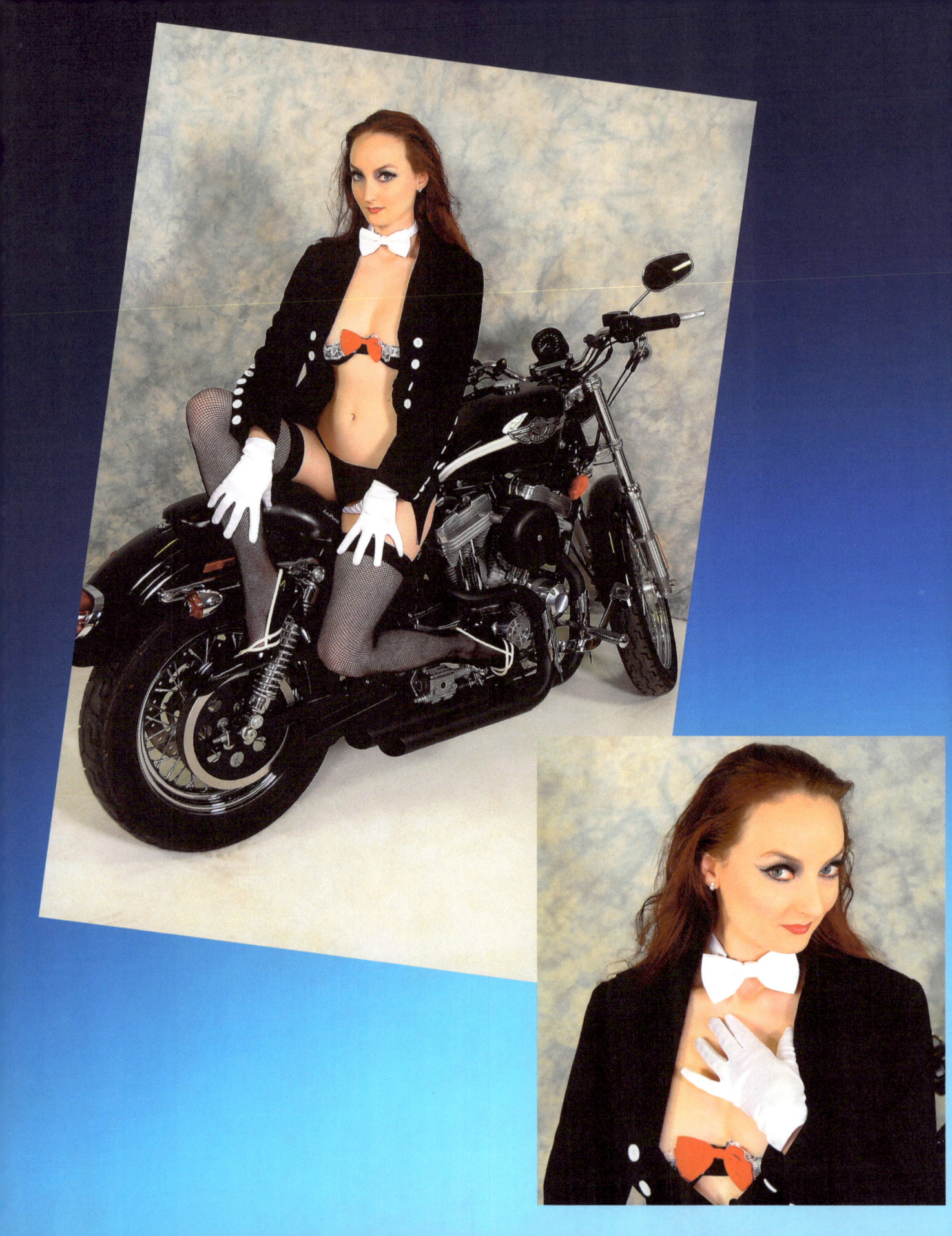

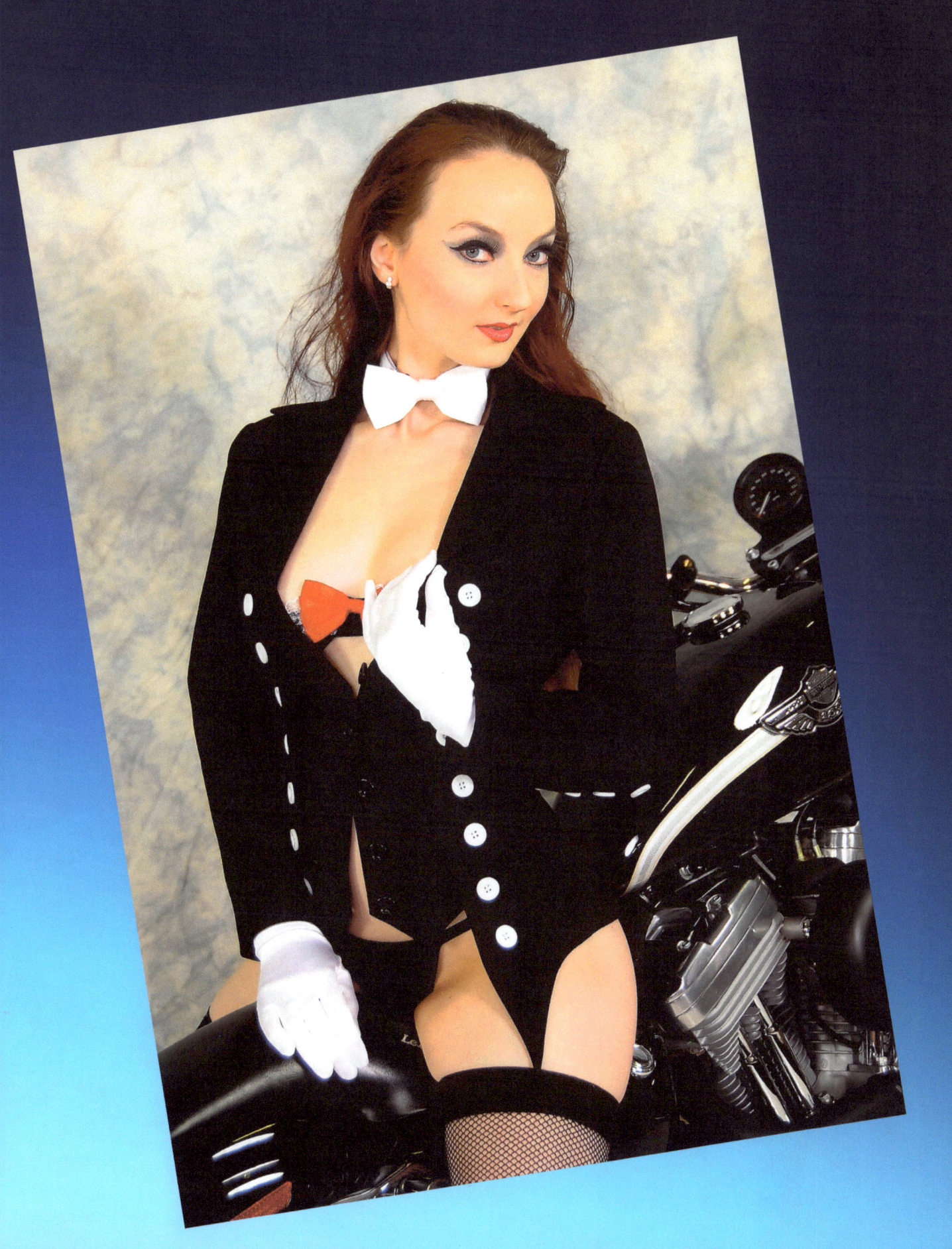

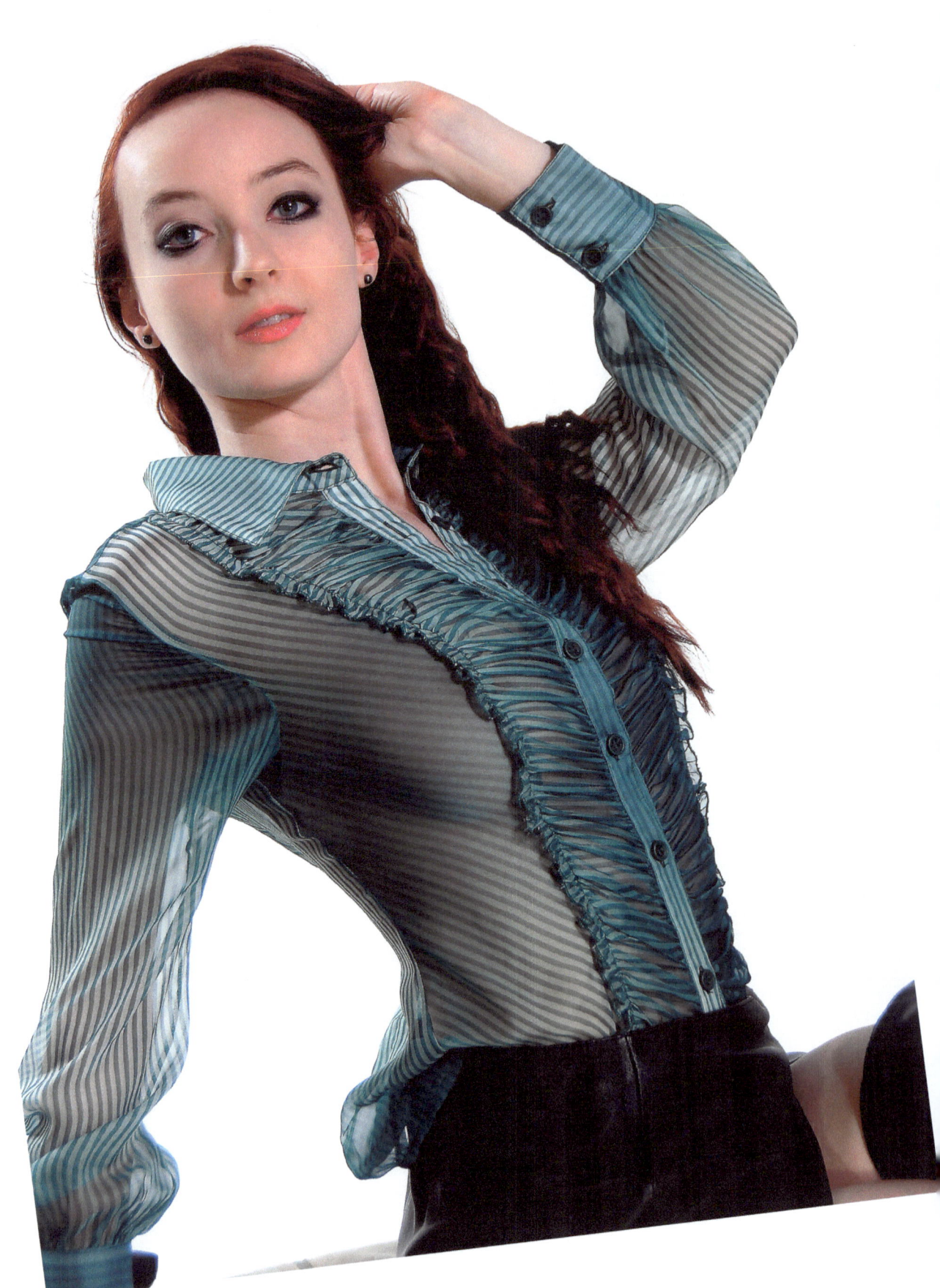

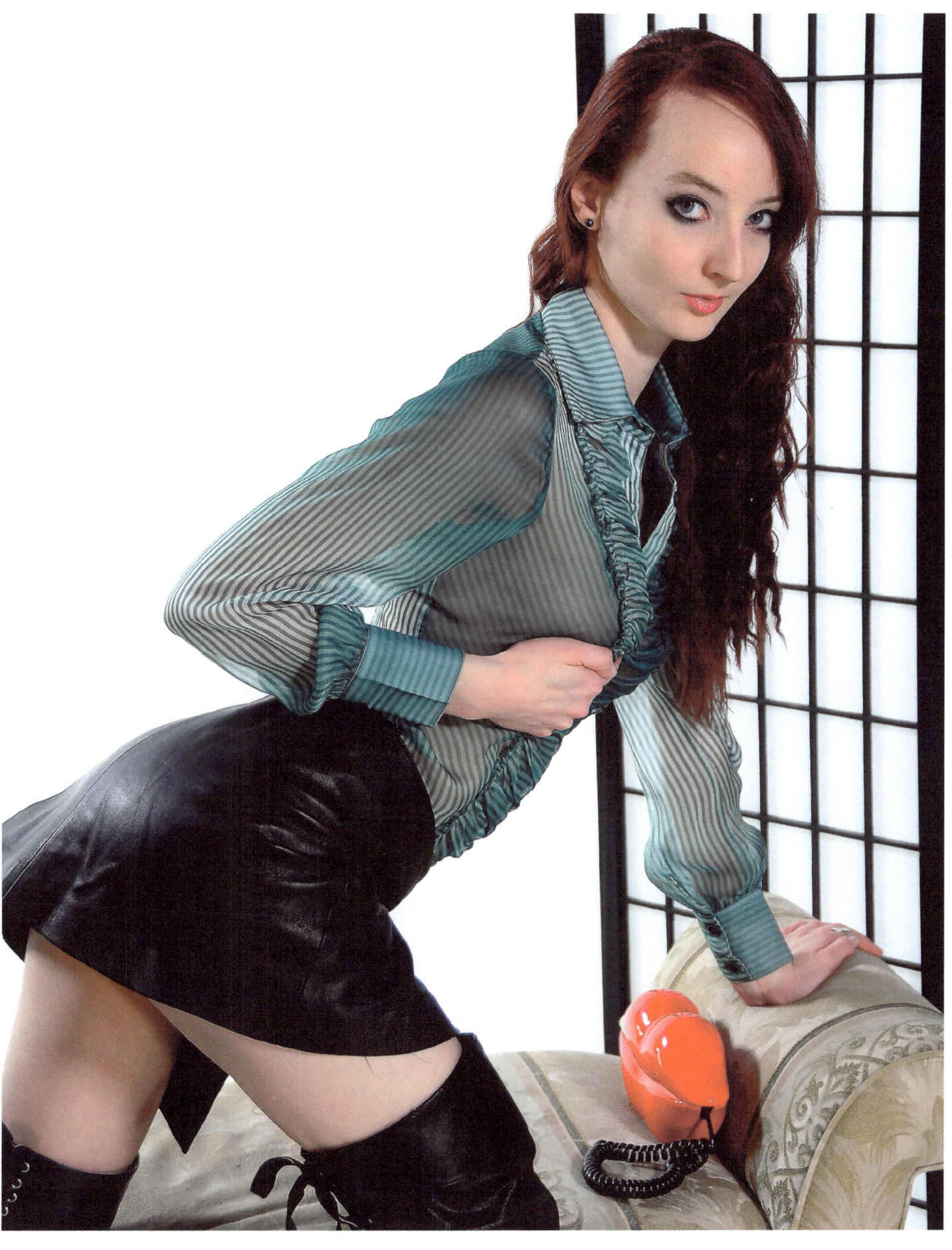

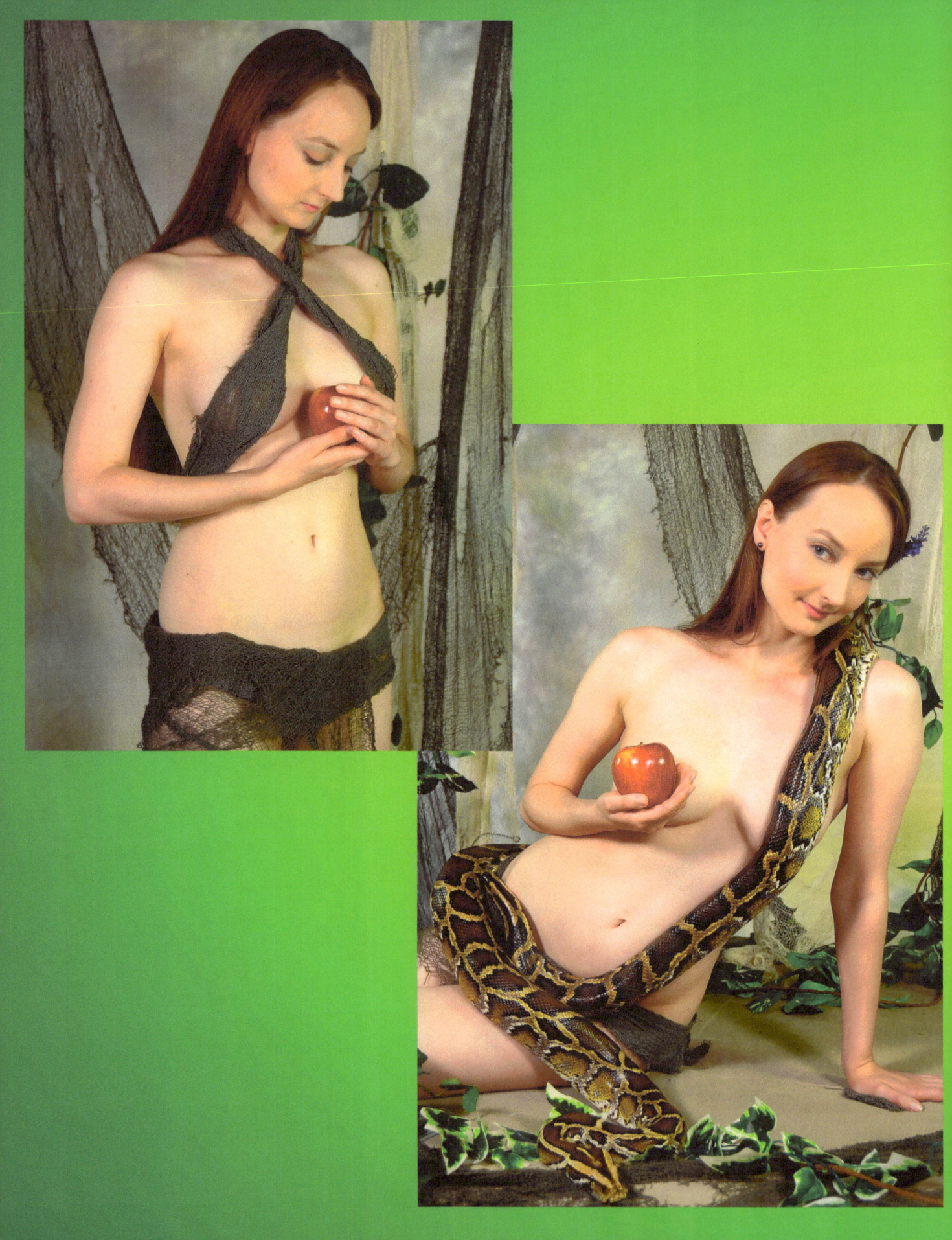

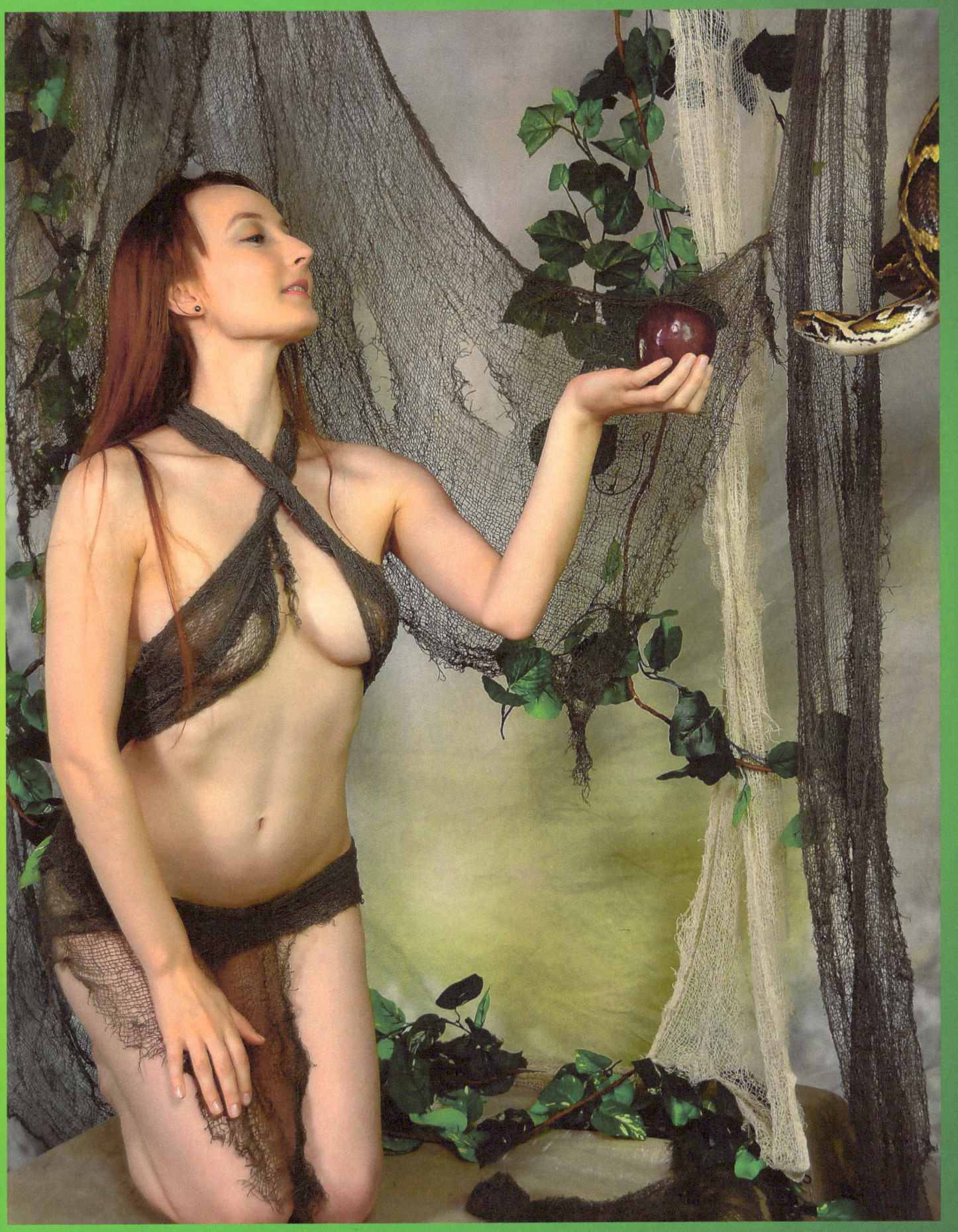

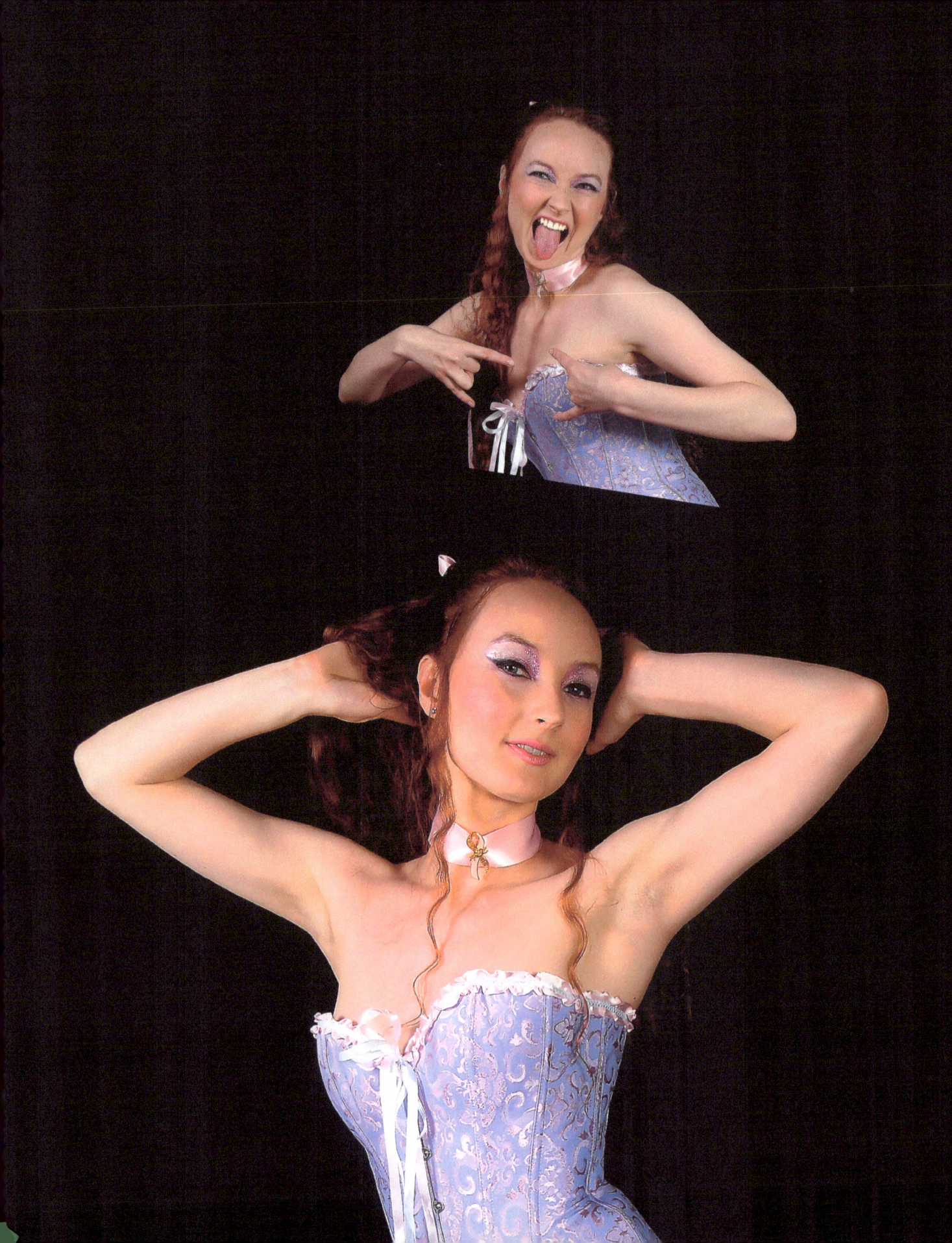

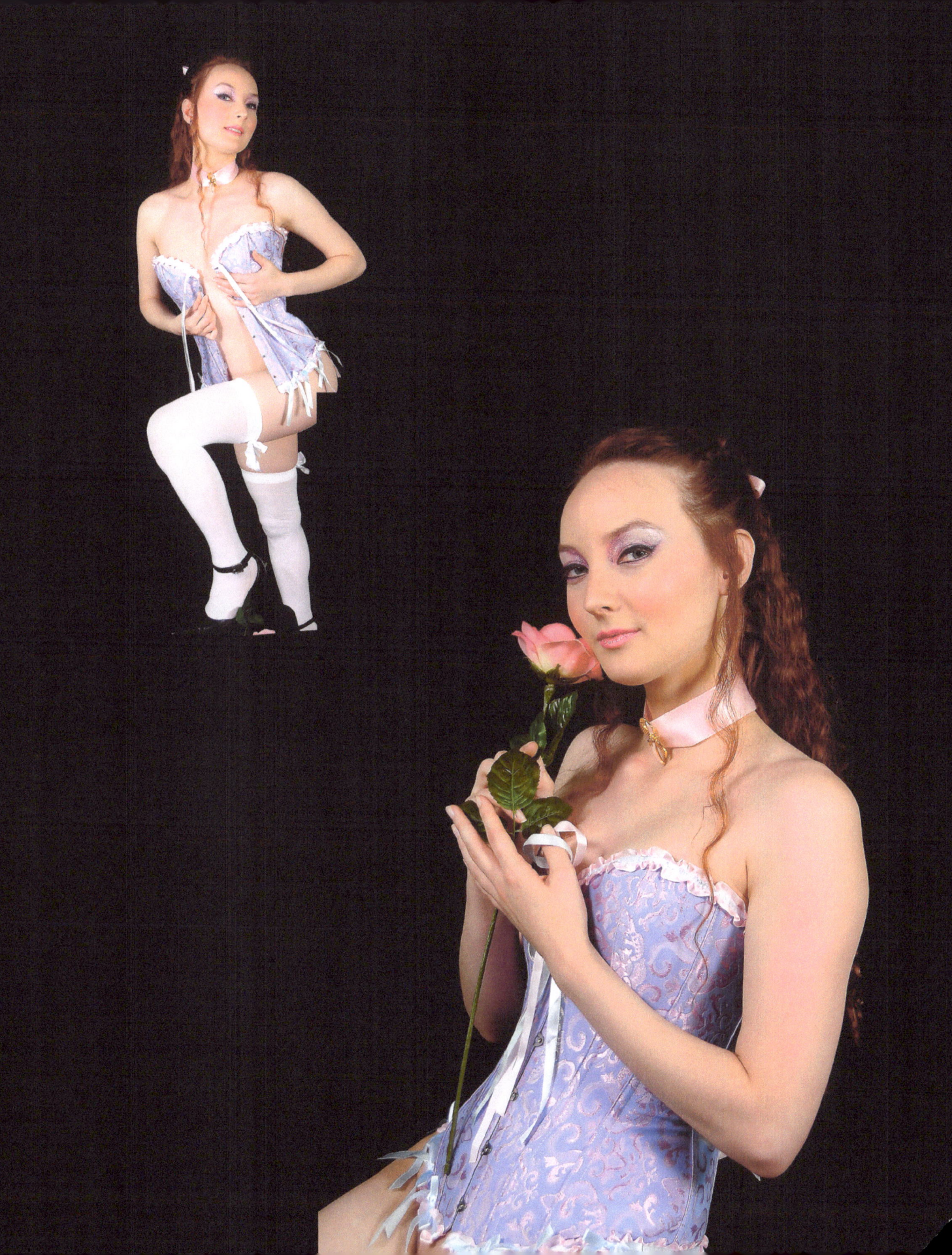

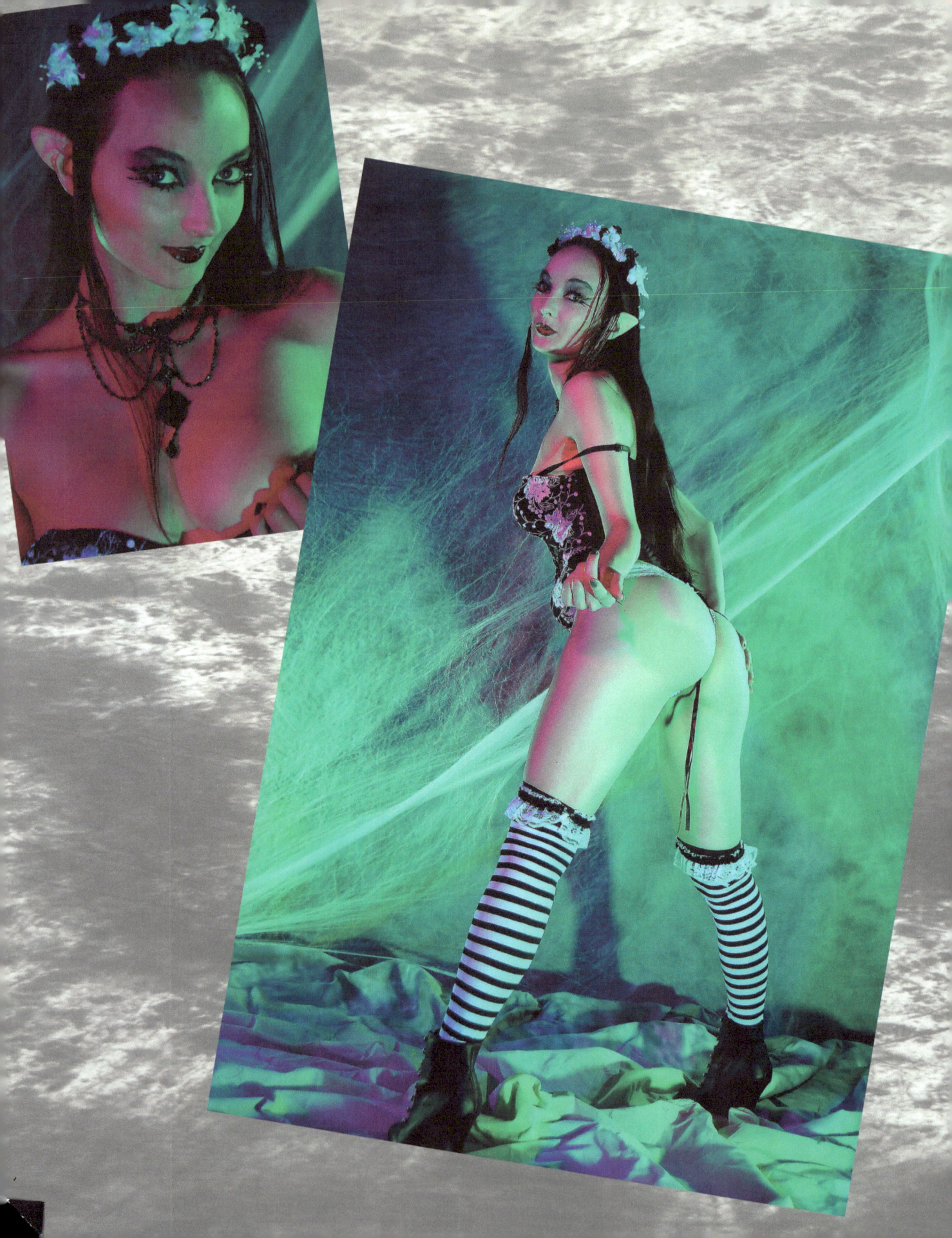

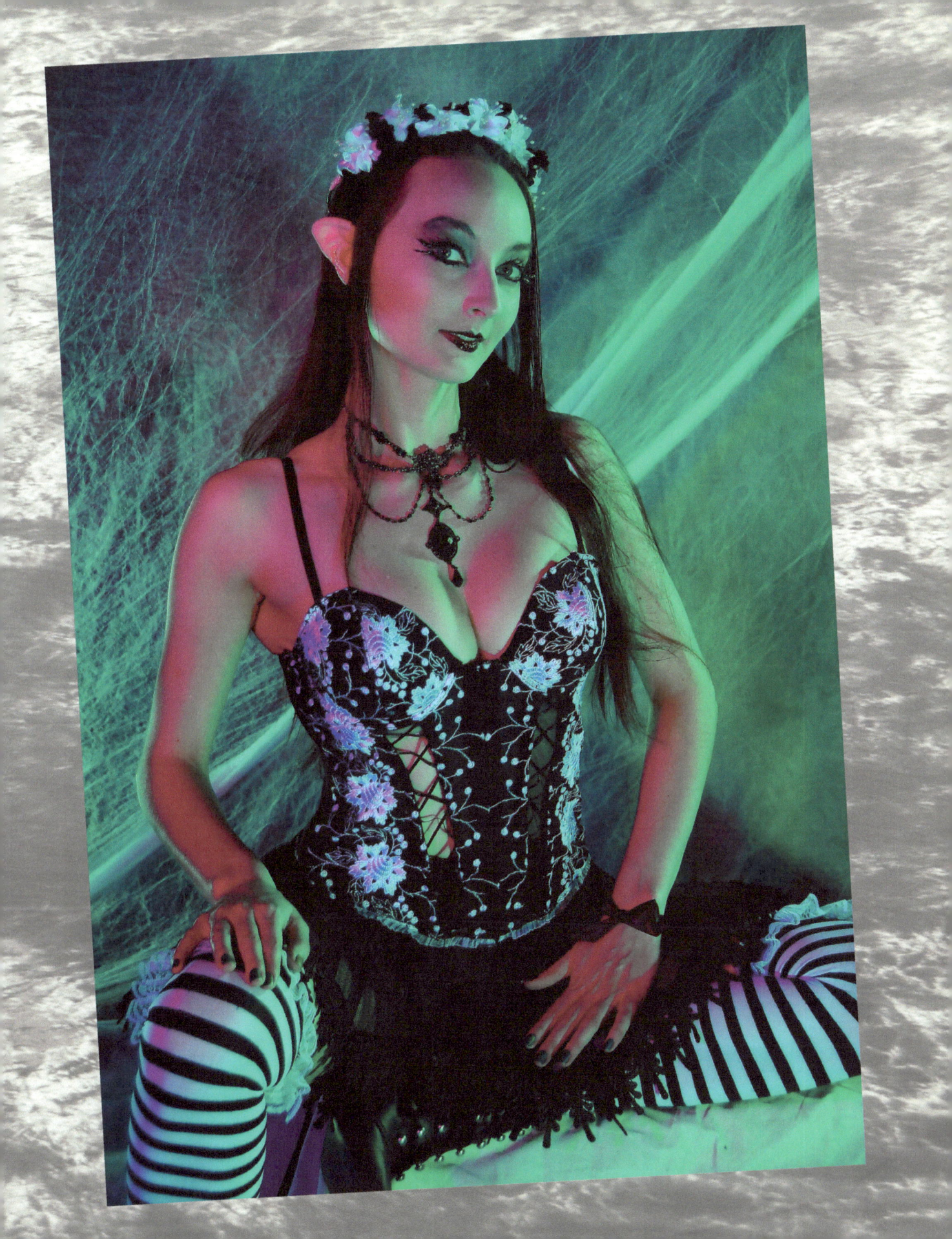

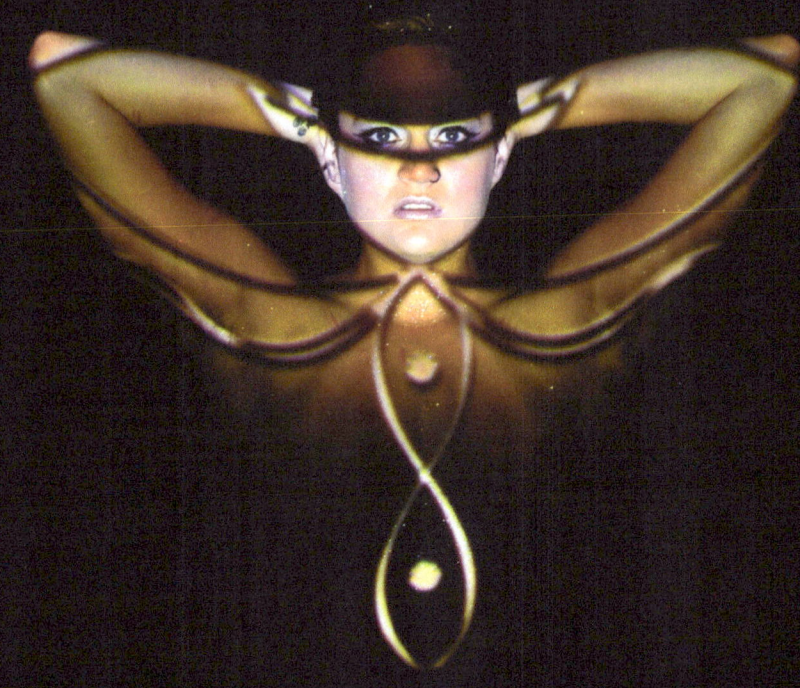
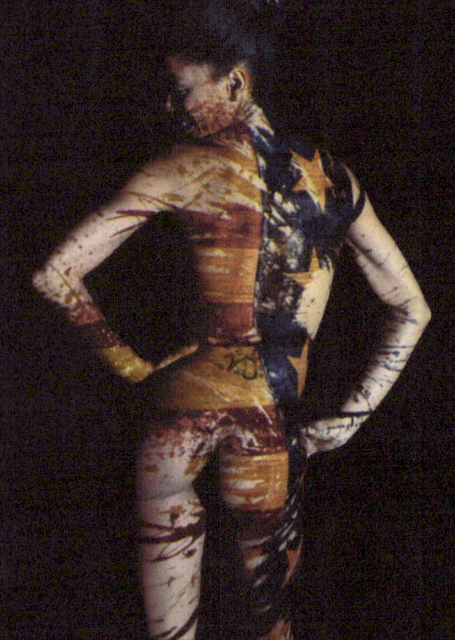
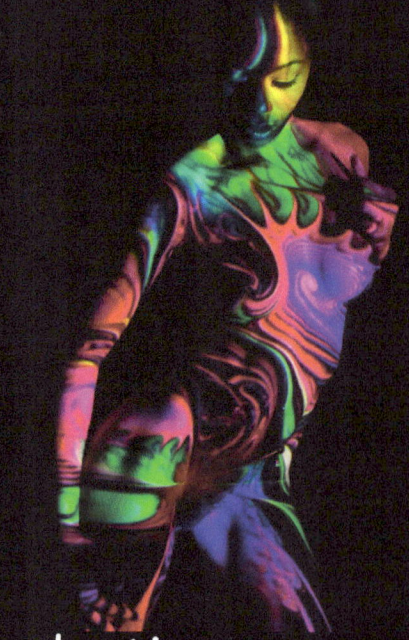

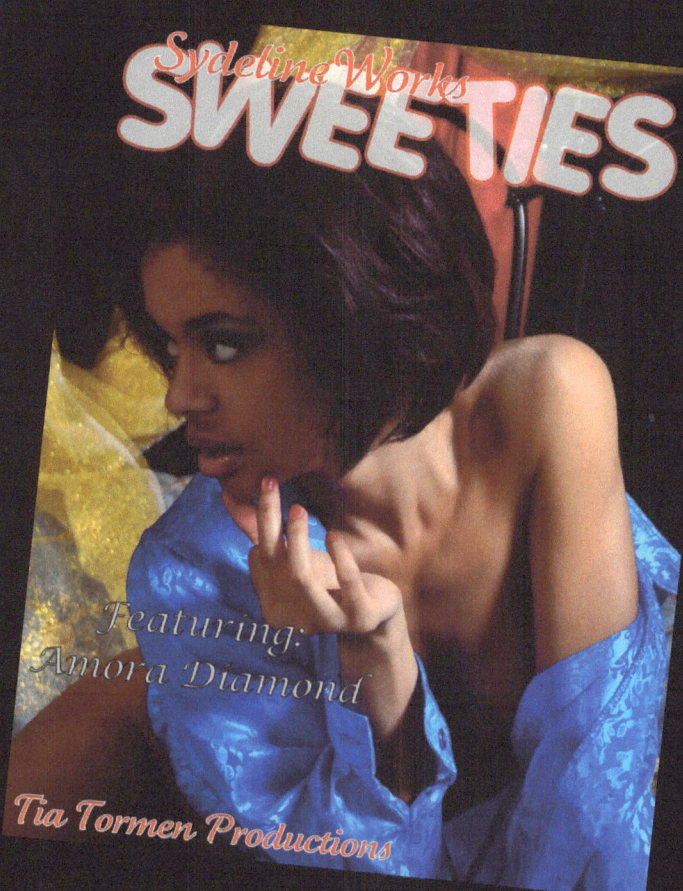

Get these other great SWEETIES and SELECT SydelineWorks titles through Tia Tormen Productions

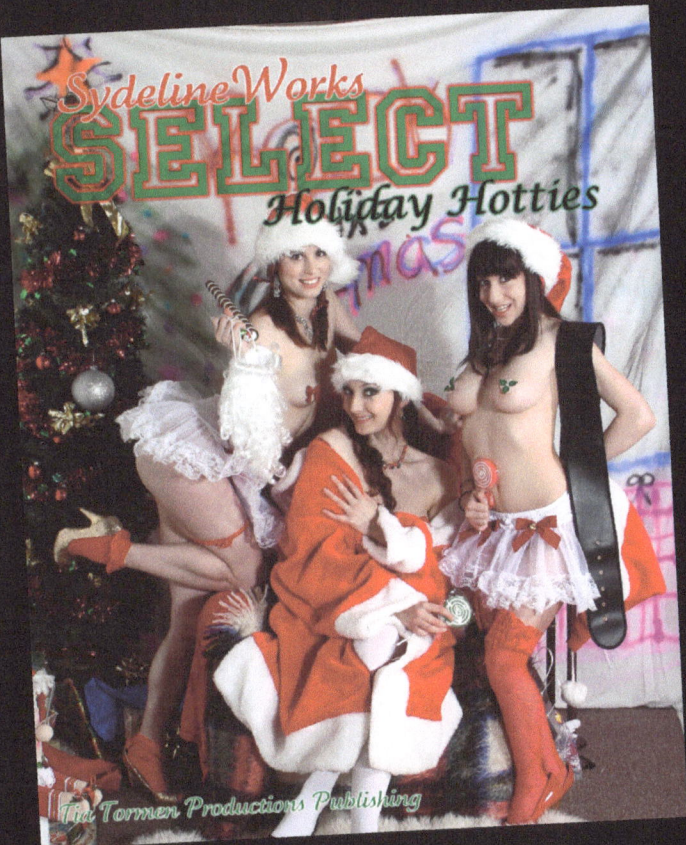

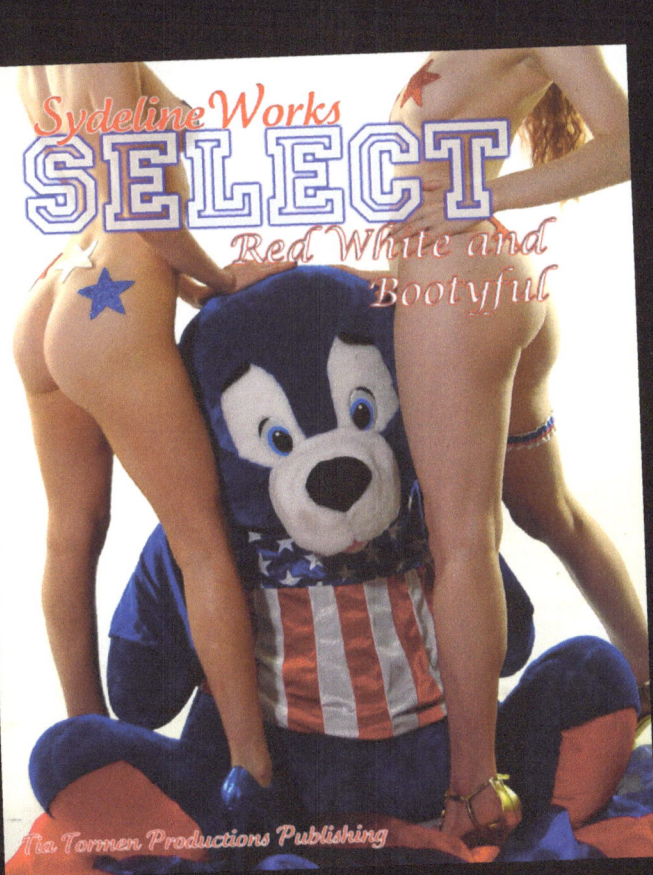

Tia Tormen Productions
P.O. Box 8069
Pittsburgh, PA 15216

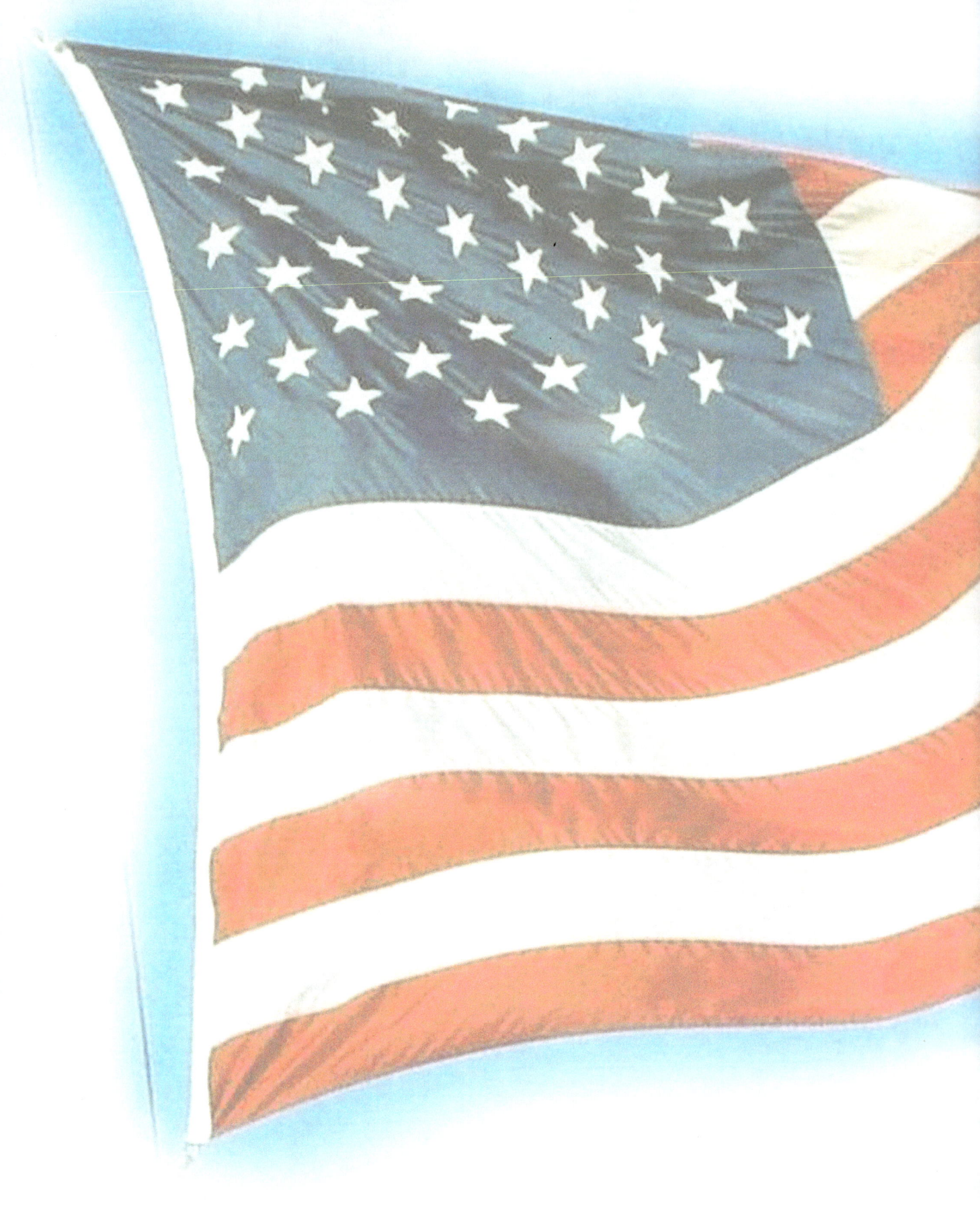

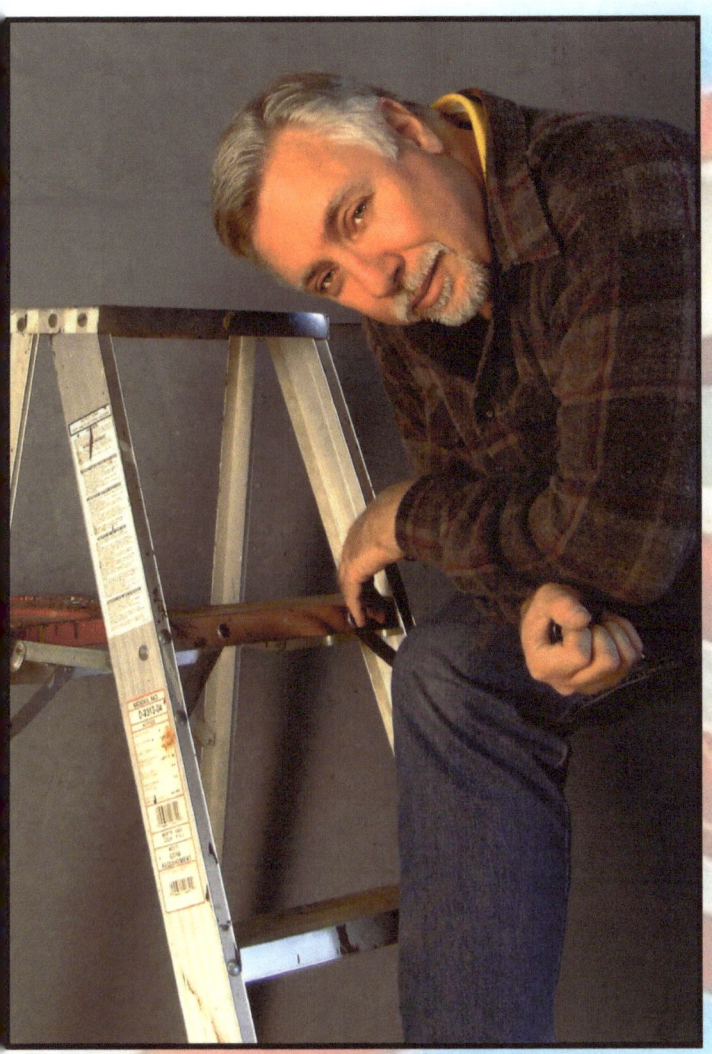

Mark Leighty is a not so typical middle-class American. A Baby-Boomer of the 50's, he attended military school during the Vietnam War and received an appointment to the US Naval Academy, but instead chose to attend a small college in the North-West region of PA

He has worked as busboy, bellhop and amusement park employee. then later became machinist welder, electrical / electronics and pneumatics / hydraulics industrial designer and fabricator. He is currently an industrial business owner and landlord.

Hobbies over the eons have included stamp collecting, genealogy, Sci-Fi books and magazines, pewter cups, figurines and other miscellaneous items, and growing Roses.

In the early 2000's he re-acquired an interest in Photography when one of his numerous children asked him to shoot their wedding photos. No longer having the equipment from his previous marriage, he started fresh in the digital age, with first Fuji, and then progressing to Nikon systems.

Looking for a change after years of capturing beloved family portraits, panoramic landscapes and fascinating architecture, he found enjoyment in photographing women, with an inclination towards Pin-Up style. It was then that he decided to start his photography hobby-company, SydelineWorks Photography.

Having the good fortune of meeting and becoming friends with the twosome of Tia Tormen and her fiancé CK Stone. His photography has blossomed to the point that publishing a book has become a reality. The opportunity of turning his unique photography styles into a paying vocation is within the realm of possibly and the next step for this near-senior citizen.

If you have made it this far through the bio, then you are either Captivated by my intriguing wit or bored. Might I suggest you go peruse the photos of the lovely, entrancing women that are enclosed within the pages of this book instead

BrittaniLuv

Hometown: Tulsa OK
Age: 26
Height: 5'6"
Measurements: 34 C, 25, 36
Describe yourself in one word: Colorful
Who is your favorite Author? Roald Dahl
What is your favorite Book? Hitchhiker's Guide to the Galaxy
My one wish: I'd wish that everyone saw themselves in a better light.
I love anything artistic. And the chance to put my dance background to use.

I'm in love
with life
with people
people who create
and people who love people who create

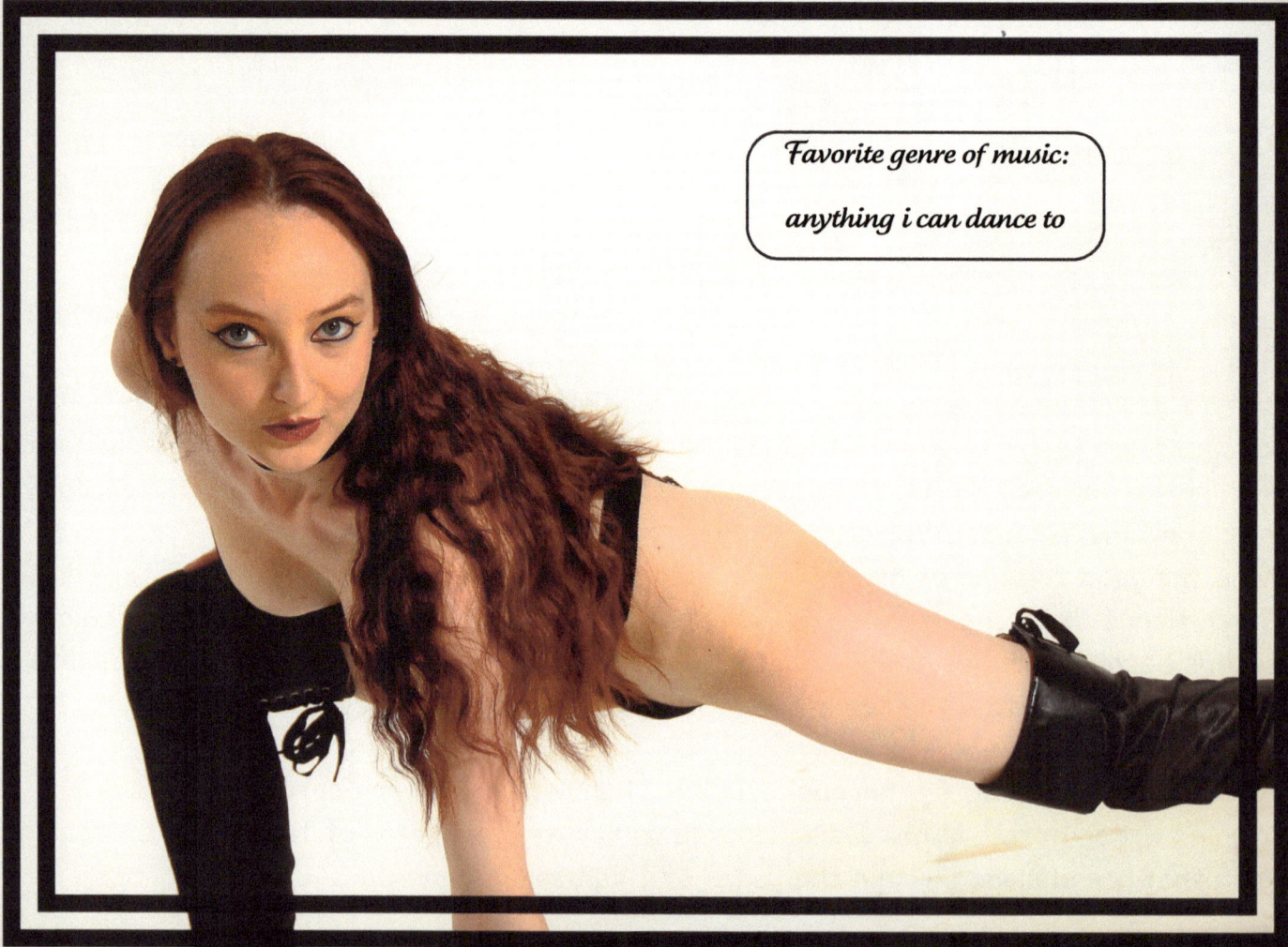

Favorite genre of music:

anything i can dance to

www.ingramcontent.com/pod-product-compliance
Lightning Source LLC
Chambersburg PA
CBHW040743200526
45159CB00023B/1629